Molly Manila

The Girl Who Talks To Animals

J T SCOTT

Molly Manila

The Girl Who Talks To Animals

Copyright © 2021 J T Scott

First published in 2021

ISBN: 9798651751006

www.mollymanila.com

J T SCOTT

J T Scott lives in Cornwall surrounded by open countryside,
lots of castles, pens, paper and a vivid imagination.

Other titles by J T Scott

Sammy Rambles

Sammy Rambles and the Floating Circus
Sammy Rambles and the Land of the Pharaohs
Sammy Rambles and the Angel of 'El Horidore
Sammy Rambles and the Fires of Karmandor
Sammy Rambles and the Knights of the Stone Cross

Bumper and Friends

Bumper the Bumblebee and Friends
Sally the Sparrow and Friends
William and Wendy the Worms and Friends
Boris the Butterfly and Friends
Chris the Caterpillar and Friends
Kirsty the Kitten and Friends
The Three Fish and Friends
Suzi the Seahorse and Friends
Sammie the Starfish and Friends

Activity Books

Boris the Butterfly and Friends Colouring Activity Book
Chris the Caterpillar and Friends Colouring Activity Book
Suzi the Seahorse and Friends Colouring Activity Book
Kirsty the Kitten and Friends Colouring Activity Book

MOLLY MANILA

FOR FRANKIE

CONTENTS

MOLLY MANILA

1

MOVING HOUSE

It was half past two on Saturday afternoon and there was a large grey removal van parked outside Molly Manila's house. The removal van along with three strong removal men had arrived at midday and Molly knew her moving house day had finally arrived.

After checking with Molly's parents what needed to be loaded and where it was going the removal men started piling all of the Manila family's possessions into the back of their grey van.

From her first floor bedroom, Molly was watching out of the double glazed window as the removal men carried dozens of large brown cardboard boxes out of her house and loaded them carefully into the van.

She watched as the van filled up with tables and chairs,

beds and wardrobes, suitcases of clothes, her bicycle, a bag full of soft toys and teddy bears.

The men were whistling cheerfully as they moved garden table and chairs, the lawnmower and a variety of tools, including a rake, fork and miniature greenhouse. They made it look easy hoisting the heavy boxes into the van.

As the last cardboard box was placed inside the van Molly shuddered. It was the third time she had moved house this year and she hoped it would be the last.

Molly heard the van doors swing shut. She saw the removal men check the doors were securely fastened and watched them walk up the garden pathway to her front door. She closed her eyes and wished it wasn't happening.

'All done,' Molly heard one of the removal men say to her parents.

'We'll meet you in Greentrees,' said another of the removal men.

As Molly opened her eyes, she saw the men climb into the cab. She heard the engine roar and then watched as the van trundled down the road. The large grey van turned the corner by the postbox and disappeared from sight.

'Are you ready Molly?' asked Molly's Mum.

Molly jumped. She hadn't heard her Mum come into her empty bedroom. She spun around and nodded.

'Your Dad and I have checked everything and we're

ready to go,' said Molly's Mum. 'Your shoes and coat are downstairs. Let's go and we'll soon be settling into our new home.'

Molly nodded again. There was a lump in her throat and she didn't trust herself to speak without choking on her words.

Yesterday she had said goodbye to all of her friends at school. They had all signed a good luck card for her. Mrs Andrews, her class teacher, had given her a gold coloured fountain pen and a spiralbound notebook with a unicorn on the front. Her best friend Ellie had given her a braided friendship bracelet in Molly's favourite colours, red, yellow and green.

Molly didn't want her parents to know she had cried herself to sleep every night since they had told her about moving house. She had wished so hard she could stay. But it was no use. Her Dad was in the Army and he had been moved to the village called Greentrees for the foreseeable future.

Molly knew her Mum was happy about the move because she could transfer her veterinary practice to Greentrees. From the sound of the new house, it was going to be big enough to have the rooms her Mum needed without needing a separate place to work. The only person who didn't want to go was Molly Manila and there was a very good reason for that.

Molly followed her Mum downstairs. She put on her shoes and coat. Both her parents looked happy. They were ready to move house.

Molly took a deep breath. 'Just one more minute please,' she said, turning her back on her parents and running upstairs to her bedroom.

The bedroom was empty. The bed and her wardrobe with all her clothes had gone. All of her toys were in neatly labelled boxes in the back of the large grey removal van. The room felt cold. It was as though no one had ever lived or played there.

'Come on Molly!' her Dad called loudly up the stairs. 'Hurry up or we'll go without you!'

'No you won't,' whispered Molly. 'Come on. Where are you? I said I was leaving today.'

Her words were met with silence. Nothing happened. There was no sign of anything or anyone.

Molly turned around and walked slowly out of her room. A tear rolled down her cheek.

'Where are you?' sniffed Molly. 'Why haven't you come to say goodbye?'

Molly reached her bedroom door. A brisk tap on the window made her look around. She saw who it was and burst into a huge smile with salty tears streaming down both cheeks.

'You've come after all,' said Molly, the words sticking in her throat as she saw all of her friends had come to say goodbye.

On the bedroom windowsill, jockeying for space, were ten brown speckled sparrows, two blackbirds, a red breasted robin and a red squirrel with a long bushy tail.

'We would never let you go without saying goodbye,' said the squirrel. He held up a paw and offered Molly an acorn through the open window. 'Plant this in your new garden and you'll always remember us.'

'And we will always remember you,' said the robin.

All of the sparrows danced on the windowsill and bobbed their heads in agreement.

'We will miss you Molly Manila,' said the two blackbirds, opening their mouths in perfect unison.

'I will miss you all,' said Molly. She took a small green handkerchief out of her pocket and rubbed her eyes.

'Come on Molly,' Molly's Dad called from halfway up the stairs. 'It's time to go.'

'I'm ready now,' said Molly. She wrapped the acorn in the green handkerchief, tucked it into her dress pocket and skipped down the stairs.

Moments later, the front door closed for the final time and Molly was sitting in the back seat of her parents car. She clutched the acorn inside the handkerchief tucked safely inside her dress pocket.

As the car pulled out of the driveway, Molly strained her eyes to see the last glimpse of her friends. The squirrel was watching from the branches of the tree outside her old bedroom window and the sparrows, blackbirds and robin were chirping from their perches on the telephone wire.

Within a few seconds her friends were out of sight and within a few minutes Molly and her parents were joining the long grey motorway away from her old home and off to find the village called Greentrees.

Molly closed her eyes and the journey passed in a dream filled with her animal friends and the games she had played in the garden with them all. She awoke two hours later when the car finally stopped.

'Are we there?' asked Molly, rubbing sleep out of the corners of her eyes.

'We are,' said Molly's Mum. 'Welcome to Greentrees.'

'You were asleep nearly the whole way here,' said Molly's Dad. 'We could hear you snoring even with the radio turned up!'

'I was supposed to be asleep,' said Molly. 'I didn't want to come. I was hoping I would wake up and it was all just a really bad dream.'

'You don't mean that,' said Molly's Mum. 'We're going

out for dinner and when we get back you'll have a new bedroom just like your old bedroom. You'll soon make friends and you start your new school next week as well.'

'There won't be time to miss your old friends and the old house,' Molly's Dad tried to reassure her.

Molly shrugged. She uncurled her right hand and looked at the small brown acorn the squirrel had given her only a few hours ago.

'I will always remember you,' whispered Molly. She took a deep breath, opened the car door and stepped out onto a tiled brick driveway.

2

ARRIVING IN GREENTREES

Molly closed the car door and looked up at her new home. It took her breath away. The house was a large, detached three storey red brick house set back from the road. Tall oak trees with dark green leaves lined the rectangular driveway. There were small bushes dotted with pink and white flowers that looked like marshmallow sweets on the branches.

There were white lines painted on part of the driveway. Molly guessed they were parking spaces for her Mum's customers. As she looked closely at the house, Molly saw that part of the ground floor appeared to be the new offices for her Mum's veterinary practice. It didn't look too bad after all.

Molly stood on her tiptoes and looked through one of

the ground floor windows. She could see rows of emerald green plastic chairs lined around the walls and a wooden coffee table in the middle of the room piled high with magazines with animals on the covers.

The blinds were drawn in the next window and Molly guessed this was a surgery room where her Mum would see customers and help their animals.

'Why don't you explore the garden?' suggested Molly's Dad. 'Your Mum and I are going to have a cup of tea and wait for the removal men to arrive.'

'Ok,' said Molly.

She walked around to the edge of the driveway where she had seen a small gravel path leading down the side of the house. The pathway had the house on one side and a large hedgerow separating their house with the house next door.

The hedge was rather overgrown with trailing branches and weeds sticking out into the path. Molly pushed some brambles aside to get through.

At the end of the path, Molly reached out to move a large spiky bramble. But as her fingers closed around the bramble it made a strange human-like noise at her.

'Oi! Gerrof!' said the bramble. 'Watch what you're doing!'

'Oh!' squeaked Molly. 'I'm really sorry!'

Then she laughed. Why was she talking to a bramble? She bent down to have a closer look.

'Oh you're a hedgehog!' she exclaimed, relieved it hadn't been a talking bramble after all.

She leaned closer and saw a small spiky hedgehog with beetle black eyes and a pink nose.

'Well I just don't know if that's good enough,' said the hedgehog. 'Here I am sitting here minding my own business and you come along and wake me up.'

'I'm really, really sorry,' said Molly. 'I'm Molly. What's your name?'

'Archie,' said the hedgehog. 'Well, actually it's Archimedes the Second, but everyone calls me Archie. Why do you want to know?'

Molly paused and scratched her head. 'I always ask animals what they're called,' she said. 'It seems like it's the right thing to do.'

'The right thing to do?' snorted Archie. 'I've never heard anything so daft in my life. The right thing to do,' he chortled.

'Well, I was hoping we could be friends,' said Molly. 'I've just moved here and left all my old friends behind.'

'That was careless,' said Archie snootily. He raised his pink nose in the air. 'I suppose you're a careless sort of girl are you?'

'No!' exclaimed Molly. 'My Dad's in the Army and we moved here. I didn't want to come. I wanted to stay in my old home with old friends, the sparrows, the blackbirds, the robin and the squirrel.'

'Well maybe you'll be lucky and you can go back there,' said Archie 'Now, if you don't mind, I would like to go back to sleep. There's a lot of noise going on around here today.'

Molly looked at Archie and turned away, a tear rolling down her cheek. 'I just wanted to make some friends,' she sniffed.

'Don't you go crying on me,' scolded Archie. 'I'm not that bad. None of us here in the garden are that bad. Or in the village either,' he added. 'If you're not a careless sort of girl and you want to be friends then I'll be your friend. Now go away and meet the others. They'll all be wanting to know who you are and how you can talk to animals.'

Archie wiggled his pink nose at Molly and curled himself up into a tight ball. He blended in so perfectly with the brambles that Molly was surprised she had seen him at all.

Molly smiled and wiped her eyes. Perhaps it wouldn't be so bad in Greentrees after all. She carried on pushing her way through the brambles, ignoring the prickles as they scratched her fingers. Suddenly, with one last push against a particularly obstinate branch, the path opened up.

Molly gasped as she saw her new garden for the first time. It started with a large patio covered in chequered slabs of raspberry and cream square stones.

On the patio there was a large rectangular wooden table with a closed-up cream parasol resting in a round slot in the middle of the table. Eight comfortable looking slatted wooden chairs surrounded the table and were neatly tucked underneath in perfect symmetry.

At the edge of the patio there were dozens of terracotta planters and flowerpots of all different shapes and sizes. Some were filled with brightly coloured flowers and others were filled with scented herbs. Molly recognised a few of the flowers and made a note in her mind to find out the names of the others.

The patio spilled into an enormous, deliciously green flat lawn, which had been carefully mown into long and neat alternating light and dark stripes all the way to a row of tall trees at the far end of the garden.

Molly had a sudden urge to stretch her legs and she jumped, hopscotch-style, across the chequered patio squares, over the flowerpots, and then she ran down the full length of the lawn at top speed.

She leapt as high as she could, clutching at one of the branches in one of the trees at the bottom of the garden and swung backwards and forwards. When the strength in her arms gave out, Molly dropped neatly onto the soft grass. She bent her knees and put her arms out to balance, just like she'd learnt in Gymnastics at school.

With another spurt of energy, Molly threw her hands on the grass and cartwheeled three times back up the lawn towards the house. She stopped, a little out of breath, and looked at the back of her new home.

On the ground floor there were several bay windows with wooden window frames painted in a deep shade of green and a set of double doors leading out onto the patio. Molly could see her parents and the removal men moving the large cardboard boxes around inside the house.

The three-story red brick building had trails of dark green ivy twisting up wrought iron drainpipes and under the wooden window ledges. Molly looked up at the large house and wondered which of the windows belonged to her new bedroom.

Seeing the window brought back memories of her squirrel friend and the acorn he had given her. Molly checked her pocket. Despite swinging from branches and cartwheeling on the lawn, the small brown acorn was still there.

She looked around, searching for somewhere safe to plant her memories of her old friends. One of the large terracotta flowerpots on the patio looked empty, almost as though it had been put there especially for her.

With another sprint, Molly dashed to the patio and checked the flowerpot. There was a small layer of soil at the bottom. Without thinking twice, Molly dropped the acorn into the pot. She scooped up some soil from a neighbouring flowerpot and patted the acorn under the earth until it was out of sight.

'Good luck little acorn,' Molly whispered. 'Grow into a big strong tree for me to remember my friends.'

A tap on the patio door broke Molly's thoughts. She spun around and waved at her Mum. The double doors swung open and Molly's Mum stepped outside.

'What do you think Molly? Do you like the garden?'

'Yes!' said Molly. 'I've met a hedgehog called Archie and planted my acorn from my squirrel friend from our old home in that flowerpot there,' she added, pointing at the large terracotta pot.

Molly's Mum smiled. It was the same smile Molly recognised from anyone she told about the way she talked with animals. No one believed a word she said about it and she had learned not to care. She knew it was real and that was all that mattered.

'Have you finished playing in the garden?' Would you like to have a look inside?' asked Molly's Mum. 'Your room is right at the top and has a lovely view of the garden.'

Molly looked again at the outside of the house. The top floor seemed really high up. She smiled. The view of the garden would be amazing. Molly followed her Mum through the open patio doors and into a large lounge area. The floor was covered in a thick cream carpet, half hidden under the cardboard boxes.

The boxes all had large white labels stuck to the top. Molly had helped her Mum write in thick felt pen the names of the rooms the boxes would need to go into. They were labelled "Kitchen", "Bathroom", "Study" and there were several boxes with Molly's name on.

Keen to help with the unpacking, Molly picked up one of the boxes with her name on it. As her Mum opened one of the boxes with "Lounge" written on the label, Molly carried her own box out of the lounge and into a long, high-ceilinged hallway with a wooden floor and wooden stairs leading up to the first floor.

Across the hallway the front door was wide open. The removal men marched in carrying more boxes. They nodded to Molly and she stepped out of their way, scuttling up the stairs and waiting at the top for her Mum.

'This is our room,' said Molly's Mum. She held open a caramel coloured wooden door with a black iron handle.

Molly looked inside. It was a large room with several of the cardboard boxes stacked on a cream carpeted floor. Her parents bed had already been reassembled. The familiar cream bedding was resting on top, ready for the sheets, pillows and duvet to be arranged.

One of the removal men came up the stairs and placed another large brown cardboard box on the floor beside Molly and her Mum.

'This box should have your curtains inside,' said the man. 'Would you like them hung up on the rails?'

'Yes please,' said Molly's Mum. 'I'm just showing our daughter around and I will make you all another cup of tea in a moment.'

Molly followed her Mum along the hallway and past more caramel coloured wooden doors with black iron handles. The doors were all open and each room had boxes stacked one on top of the other with their possessions ready to be unpacked and things put in the right places.

At the end of the hallway there was another set of stairs, slightly smaller and narrower than the main staircase. Molly skipped past her Mum. She wanted to be the first to see inside her new room.

At the top of the stairs there was another doorway. Molly pushed the door open and walked over the threshold. Her feet sunk into the soft cream carpet. The room was full of light coming from a large window in front of her. More light came in from a window on the wall behind her.

Molly grinned excitedly. She would be able to look out at the front and the back of the house all from inside her own bedroom.

Large oak beams stretched in triangles on the sloping ceiling and there was a chandelier style lamp hanging from the beam in the middle of the room. A noise above the lamp made Molly look up and she gasped.

'Mum, look!' exclaimed Molly. She pointed at the chandelier. 'There's a bird in my room!'

Molly's Mum looked up at the ceiling. 'Oh my,' she said. 'Poor little thing. I'll fetch some gloves and we can help it get back outside.'

Molly looked at the little bird as her Mum went back down the stairs. It was a blue tit, its blue and yellow body a blur as it flew around the crystals in the chandelier.

'Hello blue tit,' said Molly. She held out her hand with her palm facing the ceiling. 'Come on down. I won't hurt you.'

Molly watched closely as the blue tit started to slow down. The circles it was flying in became larger and Molly felt herself being examined by its black eyes staring suspiciously at her.

'I can talk to animals,' Molly said softly. 'That's not so strange is it? Come down and I'll help you get back outside.'

The bird flew a little closer and circled above Molly's

head. It was as though the blue tit was deciding whether to trust Molly or not.

Molly stayed still with her palm outstretched. From her experience of talking with animals, especially birds, it sometimes took a little time before they trusted her.

'I'll help you,' said Molly. Her heart skipped a beat as the blue tit slowed down and landed on her hand, its tiny feet tickling her skin. 'I'm Molly. Who are you?'

'Bob,' said the blue tit, opening his beak a tiny fraction to get the single word spoken out loud.

'Bob,' repeated Molly. 'Well, it's very nice to meet you. I'll open the window so you can get back outside.'

Without waiting for a reply, Molly strode over to the window facing the back garden and unhooked the catch. She pushed the glass until the window was half open and held her hand outside.

'Go on then,' said Molly, watching as the blue tit cocked his head at her. 'You can go outside and be free again.'

The blue tit opened his beak again. 'Thank you, Molly,' he said. 'I was stuck in there for several days.'

Molly felt a lump in her throat. 'I had bird friends in my old house,' she said to Bob. 'I'll leave the window open in case you want to come back later.'

Bob nodded and spread his wings. He tottered on his

tiny legs to the edge of Molly's fingers.

'I'll see if I can bring you some food,' added Molly, knowing her new friend was about to leave. 'Something nice.'

'Something nice would be nice,' said Bob and Molly was sure he winked at her before taking off at the exact moment Molly's Mum returned armed with the tools she thought she would need to help a small bird out of the bedroom.

'Oh,' said Molly's Mum. 'The bird has gone.'

'It's my new friend, Bob the blue tit,' said Molly. 'He'll be back.'

3

A NEW SCHOOL

After the removal men helped Molly's parents to build the beds, wardrobes, bookcases and helped to arrange the larger furniture and kitchen appliances, it was getting dark.

Molly helped carry dozens of boxes upstairs and she felt very grown up when she was allowed to unpack her things on her own.

She came downstairs for dinner. It was fish and chips bought from a takeaway restaurant in the village by her Dad.

An hour later and feeling rather full, Molly returned to her room to read. She put some seeds in a saucer and kept checking her half open window, but Bob didn't come back.

At ten o'clock Molly's Mum and Dad came upstairs.

'Lights out Molly,' said her Dad.

'Sleep well,' said her Mum.

'Goodnight,' they said in unison, just like they had said to her last night back in Molly's old room.

Sunday disappeared in a blur for Molly. She helped unpack more boxes and arrange ornaments, put up pictures, and pile books back into bookcases. She spent part of the morning with her parents in the out of town DIY store, choosing soft furnishings. Molly found two pairs of curtains with bright yellow sunflowers on she wanted for her room and her parents agreed she could have them.

An hour in the afternoon was spent in the supermarket finding food to load up the fridge and freezer with lots of different ingredients to make their own meals. They arrived home with the car boot packed full of shopping bags.

As she helped her Mum pack away the food, Molly saw her Dad take a camouflage coloured rucksack out of the cupboard under the stairs.

'Are you going away again?' asked Molly.

Molly's Dad nodded. 'I've got an important job to do but I'll be back before you know it.'

'You're always going somewhere,' said Molly.

'I'll be back soon. I promise,' said Molly's Dad. He picked Molly up, whizzed her around in a circle and put her down on her feet.

'I know. It's just that we've only just got here,' said Molly. 'You won't be here to see me start school tomorrow.'

'I'll be back soon and I'll want to hear all about it and all about the animals you've become friends with,' said Molly's Dad. He pulled the drawstring tight on his rucksack and dropped it by the front door.

'Not that you believe me,' grumbled Molly.

'Of course I believe you,' said Molly's Dad. 'I'll see you soon. Be good.'

Molly gave him a hug and went upstairs to her room. She was tired after the long day. There was still no sign of Bob the blue tit and the saucer of seeds looked completely untouched.

At ten o'clock Molly heard a van arrive. She threw back her duvet and ran to stand at her window overlooking the front of the house. A black van was parked next to her parents car. The engine was running and the headlights were on low.

Molly saw her Dad walk across the driveway and step into the back of the van. He waved and Molly waved back, even though Molly knew her Dad thought she was asleep and he was really waving at her Mum who would be standing on the front doorstep.

Seconds later the black van drove off. Molly watched until it was out of sight. She heard a faint click as the front door closed and she tiptoed back to bed wondering when her Dad would return. Sometimes it was a week, sometimes it could be a month or longer. It all depended on the work he was involved with that he never talked about.

Molly slept like a log, waking up when strands of daylight filtered through a slight gap in her brand new sunflower curtains. She rubbed her eyes and remembered where she was.

Everything was nearly in the same place as it had been in her old room. She had the same bed, the same green swirl duvet and matching pillows, the same freestanding pine wardrobe and the same pine chest of drawers beside her bed. Even the alarm clock shaped like a silver bell and the silver framed photo of her old school friends enjoying a day at the beach, was in the same place as before.

The only differences between her old room and her new room were in the way Molly's wardrobe was now facing the end of her bed and her study desk was now positioned under the window with the view looking out over the back garden.

Molly had wanted to try her desk under the window so that it was overlooking the driveway and front garden, but on her Dad's advice she had agreed she might be distracted from her studies when her Mum's clients arrived and departed with their animals on leads or in carry-cages.

Feeling excited about starting her new school, Molly threw back her duvet and found her school uniform hanging neatly in her wardrobe. She dressed at top speed then paused to tie back her curtains and check her reflection in the mirror fixed to the back of the bedroom door.

In the mirror, Molly looked at herself wearing her new school uniform. It was a plain black skirt, a crisp white short sleeved shirt and a thin red and blue striped tie. The tie was supposed to be fastened loosely around her neck. Molly wondered if the other children would be wearing ties. It felt very strange compared with wearing a navy jumper, cream tshirt and black trousers at her old school.

Molly skipped down her staircase, across the cream carpeted hallway, past her parents' bedroom and down the second flight of stairs. She found her Mum in the kitchen cooking pancakes and laying out plates, cutlery, lemon juice and sugar on the breakfast bar.

'I'm making your favourite breakfast,' said Molly's Mum. 'Would you like me to walk with you to school as it's your first day?'

'It's only at the end of the road,' said Molly. She rolled a pancake into a tube and sprinkled lemon juice on top. 'I'll be fine,' she added, taking a large bite and wrinkling up her nose as the lemon juice sprayed in her mouth.

'Very well,' said Molly's Mum. 'Will you send me a message when you get there?'

Molly rolled her eyes. 'Yes Mum,' she said, taking

another bite of her pancake.

Molly's Mum pointed at the kitchen clock. It was half past eight. 'You've got ten minutes to eat and pack your bag,' she said, 'and I've got twenty minutes before my first client.'

'Who's coming?' asked Molly, finishing her pancake and helping herself to another one.

'It's a lady called Mrs McGillam,' said Molly's Mum. 'She runs the village shop and post office. Her cat is limping and she wants me to have a look.'

Molly nodded. She knew her Mum would probably want to take an x-ray and perhaps advise buying some special cat food.

'What's her cat called?' asked Molly.

'Sheba,' said Molly's Mum. 'She's a seven year old Siamese cat.'

Molly finished her second pancake and made a mental note of Mrs McGillam and Sheba. She liked to know who was visiting her Mum's veterinary practice. Sometimes she was allowed to sit in the consultation room and at the end of the appointment, when the customer was paying for prescriptions and collecting treatments, Molly would chat quietly with the animals.

Two minutes later, Molly was wearing her lightweight school anorak. She slung her black rucksack with the

Greentrees school logo on the back over her right shoulder and opened the front door.

'I feel so overdressed,' complained Molly. 'If no one else is wearing a tie I'm taking mine off!'

Molly's Mum kissed Molly on both cheeks. 'Have a lovely day,' she said, smiling and waving as Molly crossed the driveway and set off along the pavement.

At the school gates, Molly was pleased to see her new school was quite small. It was about the size of a village hall and as she got closer to the entrance, she could see underneath the arched roof there was a white board with "Greentrees School" written in large green letters and "Greentrees Village Hall" written in smaller letters underneath. Below the smaller words was a large copper bell hanging from a large copper bracket.

The single storey building was made of red bricks and had a sloping slate roof with black guttering. Two large rectangular windows were spaced equally to the left and right of the glass double entrance doors. Beside the windows were two matching terracotta pots filled to the brim with bright orange geraniums.

The space at the front of the school formed the school playground, although it looked as though the play area stretched around the side of the building as well.

A group of four children were congregated in a corner.

There were three girls and one boy, all deep in animated conversation, waving their arms in the air and nodding vigorously at each other.

Molly noticed two of the girls were the same height and had the same colour brown hair tied in ponytails that came halfway down their backs. They were wearing the school uniform and, Molly noticed, the red and blue school tie.

The other girl was slightly taller with short blonde hair that came down to her collar and flicked out to her shoulders. The boy had blond hair and Molly wondered if they were brother and sister talking to a pair of twins.

As she made her way over to introduce herself, Molly noticed a car pull up at the school gates. It was a sleek flash of silver in the corner of her eye and she turned around. It was a silver Rolls Royce. Molly gasped. She recognised it immediately but until that moment she had no idea these cars existed outside of the pages of her Dad's car magazines.

The car purred and stopped. A young man wearing a black suit and a black peaked cap stepped out from the driver's side. He wore white driving gloves that matched his crisp white shirt. He didn't look very old. Molly watched as he stepped neatly to the back of the car and opened the rear passenger door next to the pavement.

A boy who looked about Molly's age jumped out of the car. He grinned cheekily at his driver and straightened his tie using a reflection of himself in the mirrored window.

'Thank you Mr Tomkins,' said the boy.

The driver touched his cap with his left hand and handed the boy a black rucksack, just like the black rucksack Molly was carrying.

'Have a good day Joey,' said Mr Tomkins. 'I'll be back at half past three on the dot.'

The other children in the playground stopped what they were doing and ran over.

'Hi Joey!' shouted one of the brown haired girls.

'Hi Chloe and Chelsea! Hi Jasmine and Casey!' said Joey. 'Did you have a good weekend?'

Everyone nodded and Joey turned to Molly. 'Hi there, are you new?' he asked Molly.

Molly nodded. 'I'm Molly,' she said, feeling a little nervous. 'This is my first day. We moved into Greentrees on Saturday.'

'Do you live at the Vets?' asked Joey. 'They were removing the "Sold" sign when we drove home on Friday. Are your parents Vets?'

'My Mum's a Vet,' said Molly. 'My Dad's in the Army.'

Joey nodded. 'My Mum's been looking forward to you arriving. She has horses,' he explained. 'They're always needing the Vet for something.'

Molly grinned. 'My Mum will have to visit your horses.

28

She does on-site visits. Usually the largest animals that come to her practice are dogs and cats.'

'I live at Stags Farm,' said Joey. He pointed towards a building on the hillside behind the school. 'You can come round sometime if you like.'

'That sounds great,' said Molly, jumping as the large copper bell suddenly sprang into life.

Molly put her hands to her ears as the sound clanged loudly around the playground. The double doors opened wide and a woman wearing a blue dress with white spots appeared at the door.

'Good morning!' said the woman. She held the doors open and the children ran inside.

Joey was first and Molly was last. The other children hustled inside after Joey. They were taking off their coats and hanging them on named pegs hanging on the wall just inside the door.

Molly felt a little overwhelmed as the coats were flung on pegs labelled "Chloe", "Chelsea", "Casey" and "Jasmine". There were pegs on both sides of the entrance hall and soon nearly all the pegs were full. She took off her own lightweight jacket and to her surprise, there was a peg with her name written beside it.

'You must be Molly,' said the woman at the door. 'I'm Miss Learner, your class teacher. Welcome to our school.

I'm sure you'll be very happy here. You can meet my daughter Abigale and she will introduce you to everyone in no time at all.'

Molly nodded but didn't reply. She was busy watching the door as three boys burst through the school gates and raced each other to get inside. They stripped off their coats and flung them haphazardly at the empty pegs.

'Hello Ravi, Ahmed and Robbie,' said Miss Learner. 'I was hoping you had used up all your energy at the weekend playing football and will be sensible at school this week.'

The boys grinned and nodded. Then they were racing down the corridor after the other children. They opened a door and disappeared. Molly guessed they had gone into the classroom.

'We have a small school here at Greentrees,' said Miss Learner. 'A small school in a small village. You'll soon get used to it all.'

'Thank you,' said Molly. She hung her coat firmly onto the peg with her name. 'I'm sure I will.'

4

MRS MCGILLAM'S CAT

When the copper bell rang for lunch, Molly had settled into her new classroom. She was sitting next to Jasmine at a large grey plastic topped desk. She had a comfortable grey plastic chair with room to stretch her legs under the desk and a good view of the interactive board.

For the first hour, Molly was busy getting to know her new friends. Jasmine and Casey were brother and sister and their parents ran the fish and chip shop in the village. They were excited when Molly told them she'd had fish and chips for dinner at the weekend.

'Our fish and chips are the best,' Casey assured Molly.

Joey's parents seemed to have an enormous manor house and farmland. Ravi's parents were doctors. Abigale's Mum was their teacher, Miss Learner. Robbie's Dad was a

31

policeman. Molly was good at remembering details. It came in handy when she helped her Mum with animals visiting the surgery, but sometimes she struggled when there was so much to remember at once.

Molly's favourite part of her new classroom was that her desk with Jasmine was next to the window which meant she could look out at the rest of the playground.

Hidden from the road was an area filled with swings, slides and climbing equipment. There was a tall bird feeder with multiple arms spread out holding fatballs, seed trays at different heights and a large water dish for birds to drink and bathe.

Whilst Miss Learner was talking about the topics they would be studying this week Molly watched the comings and goings at the bird table. There were families of blackbirds and sparrows taking it in turns to feed, drink and bath. But what caught Molly's eye, sitting on the top branch of the bird feeder, staring at the classroom window, was a male blue tit.

Molly watched the blue tit out of the corner of her eye. He never moved from his perch, just tipping his head occasionally, almost as though he wanted Molly to know he was there.

Molly jotted down some notes from the interactive board and nearly jumped out of her seat when the copper bell chimed again.

'Lunchtime!' said Jasmine. 'Did you bring some lunch?' she asked Molly. 'If you didn't then you can share some of mine. We always have fish sandwiches and anything that's left over from last night's cooking.'

'Thanks,' said Molly, 'but I've got sandwiches and some fruit. We can share if you like?'

'Great!' said Jasmine. 'We usually eat outside unless it's raining.'

Molly took the brown paper bag with her lunch outside to the playground. She sat on the climbing frame next to Jasmine and her new friend told Molly all about her brother Casey and how they sometimes helped their parents in the fish and chip shop, which Molly learned was called "Catch of the Day".

The boys were playing football and they called Molly and Jasmine to join them. Robbie and Joey were in opposite goals with everyone else in the class in two separate teams.

It was the quickest lunchbreak Molly had ever had as the football was passed up and down the playground. They used the climbing frame as a goal at one end and the space between the swings as a goal at the other end.

All the time they were playing Molly felt as though she was being watched. She looked around but could only see the blue tit on the bird feeder. A sudden thought occurred to Molly.

'It's Bob!' Molly said to herself. 'He's come to see me at school!' She ran forward and kicked the ball as hard as she could. The football soared through the air and landed straight in Robbie's arms.

'Try harder Molly!' shouted Robbie. He threw the ball back into play and Jasmine caught it with her right foot.

Molly was impressed as Jasmine brought the football safely into her control before she sent it flying with a sharp kick from her left foot.

Joey stuck his hands out and dived but the ball flew just beyond his reach and through the open goal between the swings.

'Yes!' shrieked Jasmine and she ran round celebrating her goal with her hands in the air like Molly had seen professional football players celebrate their goals on TV.

A few minutes later the copper bell launched itself into a tuneful melody. To Molly it was almost as though the bell was excited for them all to be returning into their classroom. They trooped back into the classroom for the afternoon lessons.

Two and a half hours vanished with Miss Learner talking about a field trip that had happened two weeks ago She asked everyone for their opinions on various animals and their habitats. Despite not being there for the trip, Molly found she knew most of the answers from conversations with her garden friends.

The copper bell rang one last time and Molly put down her pencil. She looked out of the window at the bird feeder, but it was empty. She wondered if Bob would be waiting for her at home.

Molly packed her bag and followed her new friends out of the classroom. She unhooked her jacket from her peg in the hallway and threaded her arms through the sleeves.

'I hope you've enjoyed your first day Molly,' said Miss Learner. 'You seem to be settling in very well.'

Molly nodded. 'It's been good, thank you,' she said, her eyes lighting up as she saw her Mum was waiting at the school gates and chatting with a woman who looked like a grown-up Jasmine. 'I have to go,' she said to Miss Learner.

Miss Learner smiled. 'Goodbye Molly. I'll see you tomorrow morning. Be good!'

Molly walked to the school gates with Jasmine. Casey and Joey were following them. On the opposite side of the road, Mr Tomkins was standing next to the silver Rolls Royce. Joey gave Casey a high-five and crossed the road to where his chauffeur was already opening the passenger door for him.

Molly gave her Mum a hug. 'This is Jasmine and Casey,' Molly said to her Mum. 'They're my new friends at school.'

'Hello Jasmine, hello Casey,' said Molly's Mum. 'I've been chatting with your Mum. It must be lovely having the fish and chip shop with everyone coming and going.'

Jasmine nodded. 'It is. Molly says you're a Vet. You must have lots of people coming and going as well.'

Molly's Mum laughed. 'It's good to be busy but I'd much prefer all the animals to be healthy. It's only my first day today but I've seen four people, two cats, a hamster and a dog already.'

'Have you got any more customers today?' asked Molly.

Molly's Mum smiled. 'Nothing that can't wait until tomorrow. With your Dad away I thought you might like to have the rest of the day together.'

Molly walked back up the road from the school to her house with her Mum. It was nice living so close to school and being able to walk there and back. She was looking forward to telling her Mum all about her new friends. However, when they arrived home, there was a small red post office van parked in the driveway.

'We're not expecting any parcels, are we?' asked Molly's Mum. 'I deliberately put a message on the answerphone to say there were no appointments until tomorrow.'

Molly looked at the little red van. There didn't seem to be anyone inside, but there was a large basket on the passenger seat. Just as Molly was peering into the window to see what was in the basket a lady appeared from the front porch of the house.

She was a little taller than Molly with short wavy grey hair and was wearing grey low-heeled shoes, a knee length grey skirt and matching jacket with a white shirt underneath.

'Mrs Manila,' said the woman in a broad accent. 'I hope it's no bother, but would you mind looking at my cat please? She's eaten something funny since I saw you this morning and keeps being sick.'

'Hello Mrs McGillam,' said Molly's Mum. 'Is there something else wrong with Sheba? Is she with you?'

'Yes, she is,' said Mrs McGillam. 'I've brought her in the van. I was hoping you might be able to see her today?' she said, looking first at Molly and then at Molly's Mum.

Molly's Mum nodded. 'Of course I can look at Sheba again. Bring her with you into the surgery and we can run some tests.'

Mrs McGillam looked relieved. 'Thank you Mrs Manila. Thank you so much. Sheba means the world to me. I don't know what's got into her recently. She goes out for hours at a time. I don't know where. But she always comes back when I'm ready to close the shop.'

Molly's Mum held open the side door leading into her surgery. Mrs McGillam brought the large basket from her van and laid it on the table in the waiting room. Molly noticed Mrs McGillam's fingers were trembling as she fumbled with the two catches.

'I can help,' said Molly. 'Hello Sheba, I'm Molly,' she whispered through the bars on the front of the basket as she unfastened the catches.

Two large blue eyes rolled lazily towards Molly. 'I don't care who you are,' purred the cat. 'It was worth being sick for what I've had to eat today.'

'Oh,' said Molly. She unhooked the basket door and bent down to look inside. She gasped as she saw a cream Siamese cat with large blue eyes, knowing the breed was rare and expensive. 'What did you have to eat?'

Sheba stretched her cream legs and Molly saw flashes of black on the cat's paws. She stood up inside the basket, arched her back into a long stretch, made a funny gargling noise, and threw up, just lifting her head outside of the basket so the yucky brown sick fell onto one of Molly's Mum's magazines on the waiting room table.

'Oh,' said Molly's Mum. 'Poor thing. Limping this morning and being sick this afternoon after being out all day.'

'That's right,' said Mrs McGillam. 'I don't know where she goes.

Molly's Mum picked up the magazine with the sick splodged on top and took it into her treatment room. She returned a moment later carrying a small bottle.

'Try this,' said Molly's Mum. 'Just a couple of drops tonight and a couple more tomorrow morning. See if she'll take them off your fingers or mix it in with some food. It should calm her stomach and then you can bring her back tomorrow if there's no change.'

'Thank you Mrs Manila,' said Mrs McGillam. 'I'm sorry for the mess.'

Molly's Mum waved her hand. 'Don't worry. It happens all the time.'

Molly smiled. It didn't happen all the time but Mrs McGillam didn't need to know that. She offered her hand to Sheba, hoping she could make a new friend. But the Siamese cat drew her head upright and slunk back inside the basket.

'Oh well,' Molly sighed. 'I suppose I can talk to animals but they don't have to talk to me.'

'You talk to animals and you can understand when we speak with you?' purred Sheba. She gazed intently at Molly with her bright blue eyes. 'Well, perhaps you can help me.'

'Perhaps,' said Molly cautiously. She knew from experience it was best to find out more about what animals wanted before agreeing to anything. 'What would you like my help with?'

Sheba peered out of her basket. Molly knew she was

checking to see whether Mrs McGillam was listening.

'It's ok,' said Molly. 'She's paying for the bottle of treatment. They'll be a few minutes.'

Sheba tipped her head towards Molly. 'I would like your help to clear some rubble from the bottom of Mrs McGillam's garden,' said Sheba. 'The wall is falling down and I keep stumbling on the broken bricks. That's why I'm limping today. I broke a few of my claws but your Mum has helped with that. I would prefer it didn't happen again, so I would like the bricks removed.'

'I could ask if someone could rebuild the wall,' offered Molly.

Sheba shook her head. 'No. The wall can stay down. I'm getting older and don't need to jump that high anymore. It has taken a long time to make the wall start to fall down but we didn't anticipate the bricks being left in our way.'

'We?' asked Molly. 'Who else is there?'

'Never you mind,' purred Sheba. 'Will you help me?'

'Yes,' said Molly. 'I'll need to think of something. I'll need a reason to go into Mrs McGillam's garden.'

'Her glasses,' purred Sheba. 'Tell her that her glasses are under today's newspaper. She'll invite you round to thank you and then you can arrange to remove the bricks for me.'

'I'll tell her about her glasses,' said Molly.

'Yes, her glasses,' repeated Sheba. She curled up inside

the basket and closed her bright blue eyes.

Molly fastened the two clasps on the basket. 'I hope you feel better soon Sheba,' she whispered, wondering what the cat might have eaten that upset her stomach so badly she was being sick repeatedly.

Molly's Mum and Mrs McGillam returned to the waiting room. Mrs McGillam was putting her purse into her jacket pocket.

'Are you sure I didn't leave my glasses here?' asked Mrs McGillam. 'I know I had them this morning.'

'Perhaps they're under something,' suggested Molly. 'A newspaper perhaps?'

'It's possible,' said Mrs McGillam. 'There's no harm in looking again at home. Otherwise I'll have to telephone the Optician again. They're only reading glasses but, well, you saw how I was struggling to read the bill you gave me.'

Molly's Mum nodded. 'Have another look at home.' She checked the clock on the wall. 'Give Sheba two drops tonight and two tomorrow,' she said to Mrs McGillam, holding open the surgery door. 'Let me know how Sheba is in the morning.'

Mrs McGillam picked up Sheba in the basket. 'Thank you very much Mrs Manila,' she said and with a few quick steps she was outside heading back towards her red van.

'Thank you Molly,' said Molly's Mum. 'I knew you

wouldn't mind me helping a customer. Shall we have something to eat and then when you've done your homework we can watch a film together?'

'I love animals,' said Molly, 'and I haven't got any homework so we can watch the film straight after dinner.'

Molly's Mum laughed. 'If you haven't got any homework, perhaps I should set you some!'

Molly laughed and shook her head. 'I'll probably get some tomorrow.'

A few hours later, Molly was curled up in her bed. She was full from eating the large jacket potato and baked beans from dinner, happy from watching the film, and looking forward to her second day at her new school in the morning. Her school uniform was hanging in the wardrobe and her alarm clock was set for half past seven.

Molly turned onto her side and closed her eyes. Then she opened them again. There was a noise in her bedroom. A faint noise, but definitely a noise. She reached over to turn on her bedside light. The lamp gave off a soft glow and Molly held her breath, listening intently for the noise to happen again.

After a short pause, there it was again. A small snuffling, munching noise coming from near the window that overlooked the back garden.

Molly swung her legs out from under her duvet and

dropped her feet into her slippers. She tiptoed across to the window, hoping the noise was coming from the small saucer of seeds she had rested on the windowsill.

Gently, Molly swung back the curtain. She grinned. Bob the blue tit was bending over the saucer, helping himself to the seeds.

'Hello Bob,' said Molly. 'I knew you'd come back!'

Bob looked up, tilting his head to look at Molly with one of his bright black eyes.

'I said I would,' chirped Bob, his mouth full of sunflower seeds. 'Did you have a good first day at school?'

'Yes thank you,' said Molly, and she told Bob all about her new friends.

'You'll soon have lots of friends here at home as well,' said Bob. 'I'll introduce you to them all.'

'Thank you said Molly. 'I've met Archie and you, but that's all so far.'

Bob gave a small chirrup that sounded like a laugh. 'There are lots of us here in the garden if you know where to look.'

Molly giggled as Bob did a little dance to flip a sunflower seed from the saucer into his beak. The blue tit chomped on the sunflower seed, then he turned to Molly with a serious look in his black eye.

'I saw you met Sheba and Mrs McGillam earlier,' said

Bob. 'You must watch out for that cat. She might have hidden those glasses on purpose just so she could tell you where they were and then before you know it, you're doing something for her that you had no idea about.'

Molly's eyes widened. 'Sheba told me about the glasses so I could help Mrs McGillam.'

Bob dipped his head. 'I hope so. But Sheba has a bit of a bad reputation. I wouldn't trust her. She would rather eat me and my family than say hello.'

Molly nodded. 'Cats do chase birds and eat them,' she admitted. 'It's what they're known for.'

Bob gave a slight sniff. 'Well, I don't want to be eaten by a cat,' he said loudly. 'Thank you for the sunflower seeds Molly Manila. It is time for me to return to my nest. If I were you, I would take an umbrella tomorrow morning. It's going to rain.'

'Thank you Bob,' said Molly, smiling at her bird friend. 'Good night.'

'Good night Molly,' said Bob. He spread his wings and took off into the night.

Molly tried to see where he went, but it was too dark. Wondering what Bob had meant with his warning about Sheba, she got back into bed. She wrote a couple of lines in her journal, then turned out the light and closed her eyes.

5

THE CATS ARE GETTING SICK

Molly woke to the sound of rain thumping against her bedroom windows. She rubbed her eyes, remembering where she was, and got out of bed. Molly put on her slippers and went to stand by the window.

Rain was coming in the gap in the window where she had left it ajar for Bob. Sunflower seeds were floating in the saucer which had filled up with water.

'You were right Bob,' Molly said out loud, even though no one was in the room with her. 'I will definitely need my umbrella today.'

A few minutes later Molly's bedside alarm started chiming and she got her school uniform out of the wardrobe to put on. She dressed quickly, checked her school tie in the mirror and skipped downstairs to meet her Mum and have breakfast together as usual.

'Did you sleep well?' asked Molly's Mum. 'Do you like our new home?'

'Yes and yes,' said Molly. She gobbled her cereal at top speed, gulped down a cup of lukewarm tea and loaded her bowl and mug into the dishwasher.

'Would you like me to walk to school with you this morning?' asked Molly's Mum. 'I'd be interested to meet more of your friends.'

'Ok,' said Molly, rolling her eyes. 'If you want.'

Molly's Mum laughed. 'I do want to meet your friends. I thought you might like to invite some of them here for dinner later this week.'

'Yes please,' said Molly. 'Please may I invite Jasmine, Casey and Joey?'

'Of course but do it discretely otherwise everyone in your class will want to come,' Molly's Mum laughed. 'Perhaps we can have a larger party for your birthday in the summer.'

Molly fetched her shiny black leather shoes from the shoe rack by the front door. Her eye caught a glimpse of her Dad's umbrella and she remembered Bob's warning that it would rain throughout the day. She picked up the umbrella. It was a little dusty and reminded her of her Dad.

'When will Dad be back?' Molly asked her Mum.

'Next week, just for a few days, then he's going to be away for two weeks,' said Molly's Mum. 'It was going to be a surprise.'

Molly folded her arms across her chest. 'I don't like surprises,' she said. 'Moving house was a surprise and I didn't like that.'

'But you have new friends here,' said Molly's Mum. 'Greentrees is going to be a good place for us all to live. Why have you got that old umbrella today?' she asked, spotting the umbrella tucked under Molly's arm.

'It's going to rain today,' said Molly, uncrossing her arms and putting her hands on her hips. 'Bob says so.'

'It finished raining half an hour ago,' said Molly's Mum. 'Take it if you wish. Are you ready to go?'

'Bob said it was going to rain,' Molly whispered under her breath. She pulled open the front door and checked the weather outside the porch.

It was dry. The shower from earlier in the morning had stopped, but there were heavy rainclouds in the air. Molly skipped across the driveway and waited for her Mum to lock the front door and join her on the pavement. They walked down the road to the school.

Joey's silver Rolls Royce was parked at the school gates. Molly's Mum went to the driver's window and introduced herself. Molly could hear her Mum inviting Joey for tea on

Friday afternoon. She saw his driver nod and make a note on a tablet.

Next Molly's Mum turned to Mrs Cooper who had just arrived with Jasmine and Casey.

'Would Jasmine and Casey like to come round for dinner on Friday?' asked Molly's Mum.

Mrs Cooper nodded at once. 'That would be lovely,' she said. 'We can invite Molly over for fish and chips at ours the week after.'

'And she can come to mine,' added Joey. 'We can go horse riding in the woods.'

'That would be lovely,' said Molly's Mum. 'It would give me a chance to speak with your parents about the horses.'

'They always need looking after,' said Joey. 'We've also got sheep and deer. Our estate is over a hundred acres.'

'Wow,' said Molly, touching her hair as she felt spots of rain. 'A hundred acres.'

'More than a hundred acres,' said Joey. 'But it's not as cool as having a Vet for a Mum or owning a fish and chip shop.'

'Or having a teacher for a Mum,' said Abigale.

'Or a Police Officer for a Dad,' added Robbie.

'Here, said Molly, offering her Mum the umbrella as spots of rain started tumbling down from the sky.

Molly's Mum opened the camouflaged patterned

umbrella and laughed. 'You told me it was going to rain,' she said to Molly. 'Hurry into school and I'll be back later to meet you.'

Several hours later it stopped raining. Molly enjoyed her lessons but was glad when it was time to go home. She packed her pens and paper into her rucksack and looked out of the classroom window to see if her Mum was at the gates. She couldn't see her, but there was a camouflaged coloured umbrella bobbing its way down the road towards the school.

Molly skipped down the school corridor and unhooked her coat off the peg. She waited for Jasmine, Casey and Joey and they walked up to the school gates just as her Mum arrived.

'We've had a phone call today Molly,' said Molly's Mum. 'Mrs McGillam found her glasses exactly where you suggested and she wants us to go round to the post office tomorrow after school to have coffee and cake in her house behind the shop front.'

'I don't like coffee,' said Molly. 'I was only making a suggestion where her glasses might be,' she added, crossing her fingers behind her back. Really, she had believed every word Sheba had said. At the back of her mind, Molly also remembered Bob's warning about Sheba.

'I'll drink the coffee,' said Molly's Mum. 'You can eat the cake and make sure Sheba is better. I was a little worried about the colour of Sheba's sickness. I've seen something like it before, but I really hope it isn't that.'

'Isn't what?' asked Molly.

Molly's Mum shook her head. 'Nothing. I'm sure it's nothing.'

'Do you mean poison?' asked Molly, her eyes wide. 'Do you think someone's poisoned Sheba? Who would do something like that?'

'Well, the thought had crossed my mind,' said Molly's Mum. 'But I can't imagine that would happen in somewhere like Greentrees.'

'Maybe someone doesn't like cats,' suggested Molly. 'I'll come with you after school tomorrow and find out.'

Molly's Mum chuckled. 'Well I'm glad you'll come with me, even if it's for the strangest of reasons. I can't honestly think anyone is trying to poison the post office cat.'

Whilst eating dinner and watching TV Molly thought about Mrs McGillam and wondered whether it was possible someone wanted to poison her cat. A disgruntled customer perhaps. Or one of her neighbours. Molly felt her eyes closing and she was glad when her Mum prodded her and said it was time for bed.

Mrs McGillam's cat was the topic of conversation at breakfast the following morning. Molly had drawn up a shortlist of suspects, but her Mum dismissed the idea straightaway.

'I really don't think someone would deliberately do that,' said Molly's Mum. 'Not around here.'

Molly shrugged and picked up her rucksack. 'I'll walk to school myself today,' she announced. 'I know you've got a client at half past eight.'

Molly's Mum nodded. 'I'm meeting Lady Baxter, Joey's Mum. She has several horses and wants to register their details on my system.'

'I know,' said Molly. 'Joey told me his Mum wanted to see you. He's invited me round to his house as well.'

'That's good,' said Molly's Mum. 'Do you know when?'

'Whenever,' said Molly, swinging on the front door. 'I'll see you later,' she swung away from the door handle, hugged her Mum, and skipped across the driveway, waving as she disappeared down the road.

The day passed quickly and Molly felt as though she was putting her coat back on almost as soon as she had taken it off. Her head was spinning with the maths problems, learning the capital cities, trying to memorise the dates of the reigns of Kings and Queens.

She had played football in the playground, scuffed her shoes and lost her hairband. All in all, a good day Molly thought as she left the school building with Joey, Jasmine and Casey.

'Hello Molly, hello Joey, hello Casey, hello Jasmine,' Molly's Mum greeted Molly and her friends.

'Hello Mrs Manila,' they chorused.

'Hello Mum,' said Molly, her cheeks an embarrassed shade of pink. 'You're here early.'

'We're going to see Mrs McGillam,' reminded Molly's Mum. 'For coffee,' she added with a smile.

'Oh yeah!' exclaimed Molly. 'I'll see you tomorrow,' she said to her friends and linked arms with her Mum as they walked down the road and into the village square.

Several cars passed them, including Joey and Mr Tomkins in the silver Rolls Royce. Joey waved as they drove past.

It was the first time Molly had seen the village square and it was as impressive as her friends had told her.

There was the smart white police station with its blue front door and blue light inside the iron cage above the door. Molly remembered this was where Robbie and his Dad lived, in the flat above the police station. In one of the first floor windows, Molly could see a teddy bear wearing a blue jumper with a white cross pattern facing with its head towards the street.

Next to the police station was the bakery. Molly knew it was the bakery because of the brown and white striped awning and the words "The Old Cob" written in curly writing on the large shop window.

She peered in the window and gasped. As well as row upon row of freshly baked loaves of many shapes and sizes there was a display counter filled with brightly coloured cakes.

'Can we go in there?' asked Molly, pulling her Mum towards The Old Cob. 'My friends Chloe and Chelsea Miller live there.'

'Crusty and Crumbs,' said Molly's Mum.

'What?' asked Molly.

'The Millers have two Old English Sheepdogs called Crusty and Crumbs,' explained Molly's Mum. 'Gordon Miller telephoned me this morning and he's bringing them round next week for a check-up. It sounded as though they may have been sick like Sheba.'

Molly's eyes widened. 'So, someone could be poisoning all the cats and dogs in the village,' she said. 'That's terrible.'

'There's probably a simple explanation,' said Molly's Mum, but she didn't sound very convinced.

'Probably,' said Molly, swinging her head from left to right as she looked at the other shops in the village square.

The post office where Mrs McGillam and Sheba lived was easy to find. The glossy red symbol with gold writing stood out like a beacon and there was a large red post box by the glass front door.

There was a butchers shop, the doctors surgery, a bank, a pub, a hairdresser and a greengrocer. Next to the greengrocer was "Catch of the Day", the fish and chip shop where Casey and Jasmine's parents served hot food every lunchtime and evening.

'There are a nice lot of shops for a small village,' said Molly's Mum. She headed towards the post office.

'It's bigger than you think,' said Molly, catching sight of a small blue and yellow bird whizzing up the street. 'Bob? Is that you?' asked Molly, watching as the tiny bird flew off towards her house.

Molly's Mum knocked on the post office door. There was a scurry from behind the counter and Mrs McGillam appeared. She unlocked the door and changed the sign from "Closed" to "Open".

'I'm sorry to keep you waiting,' said Mrs McGillam. 'I was just on a telephone call to my sister. 'She hasn't been well either.'

'I'm sorry to hear that,' said Molly's Mum. 'You haven't kept us waiting. We've only just arrived.'

'Come in and make yourselves at home,' said Mrs McGillam. 'I'll put the kettle on. My son is staying with me for a few days so he will look after the shop counter while we chat in the back room.'

Mrs McGillam turned to the magazine rack and, using a

hidden handle, opened a hidden door that led into her house in behind the shop front.

Molly and her Mum followed Mrs McGillam into a homely lounge with a round coffee table and cream fabric sofas lining the walls.

There was a bowl of fruit on the table with the parish magazine, a telephone handset and a half drunk cup of tea. A small television was in the corner of the room, half obscured by a palm tree standing in a pot. A man stood up as they walked in.

'I'll look after the front Mum, he said. 'Take as long as you want.' He drank the last drops of the cup of tea. 'The kettle has just boiled and I've put some biscuits on a plate for you.'

'Thank you Luke,' said Mrs McGillam. 'He's forty and just come home for a few weeks,' she explained, bustling her way into the kitchen.

There was a tinkling of china and Mrs McGillam emerged with a tray filled with two steaming cups and a plate of biscuits.

'Would you like a drink Molly?' asked Mrs McGillam.

Molly cast her eye at Sheba who was watching intently. The Siamese cat approached Molly, walked past her and stood beside patio doors leading to the garden.

'I'm ok, thank you,' said Molly. 'May I go into your

garden?'

'Of course,' said Mrs McGillam. 'The door is unlocked.'

Molly was sure Sheba winked at her as she crossed the lounge and opened the double patio doors.

Mrs McGillam's garden was a little on the wild side, with weeds growing through the gravel on the path. Overgrown bushes made the garden feel like a cave. Molly pushed her way through the bushes to the grass and the surrounding wall Sheba had described.

Straightaway, Molly could see the part of the wall that had fallen in. She lifted a couple of the bricks and put them back into place. Molly stood on tiptoe and over the top of the wall she could see fruit trees with apples and pears hanging from the branches.

Large brambly blackberry bushes were climbing up the wall and into Mrs McGillam's garden. Under the bushes Molly could make out scraps of metal, a broken garden fork and a rusty lawnmower with one of the wheels missing.

'I wonder who lives there,' Molly said out loud to herself. 'Somebody who likes fruit but doesn't care to keep their garden tidy.'

Molly looked closely at the rusty lawnmower and saw a clump of white attached to it. Feeling curious, she lifted her leg over the wall and jumped over. She bent down next to the lawnmower and saw it was white fluff and fur.

'Sheba,' whispered Molly and she knew straightaway that Sheba's limp had come from jumping over the wall and landing on the lawnmower. 'Silly cat,' she muttered.

Molly stood the lawnmower back upright, turned around and climbed back over the wall.

It was only when Molly got back home after the visit to Mrs McGillam's house was over she remembered as well as finding out how Sheba had got her limp she had been supposed to be finding out what was making the village cats and dogs sick.

Molly filled up the saucer on her bedroom windowsill with sunflower seeds. Within seconds Bob arrived. He hopped up and down waiting impatiently for her to finish. He pecked Molly's fingers gently with his beak.

'How was your day Molly Manila?' asked Bob, his blue tit sing-song voice breaking the silence. 'Did you find out why Sheba has been sick?'

Molly shook her head. 'I found out why she's limping. She couldn't jump down from the wall without hurting herself on some machinery in the garden over the wall.'

Bob gave a small nod. 'I knew you'd find out,' he chirped triumphantly. 'There is always a simple explanation.'

'But she's a cat,' said Molly. 'She should have perfect balance and be able to jump anywhere she wants.'

Bob cocked his head. 'I agree Molly Manila,' he said

earnestly. 'But what if she was feeling sick at the time or if she was distracted by something in mid-jump?'

'Mid-jump,' repeated Molly. 'I suppose it's a possibility. Perhaps the wall gave way while she was jumping and she mis-timed her jump because of it?'

Bob nodded his tiny head enthusiastically. 'You might be right Molly Manila. That would make sense.'

Molly yawned and nodded. 'I suppose it would,' she conceded. 'I've mended the wall and moved the lawnmower out of the way. Now all I have to do is find out what she's eaten that's made her sick. Did you know Crusty and Crumbs from The Old Cob have been sick as well?'

'No,' said Bob. 'But I haven't seen them out for their walks as usual. They're lovely Old English Sheep Dogs. They shed their coats and we use the thick warm hair as lining for our nest.'

Molly smiled at the thought of Bob and his family following the dogs, spotting the stray hairs falling and scooping them up in their beaks to line the family nest.

She yawned again and got ready for bed. She closed her eyes and her last thoughts before she fell asleep were of a Siamese cat called Sheba and two large Old English Sheep Dogs called Crusty and Crumbs.

6

MIDNIGHT

Molly woke to the sound of her Mum climbing the stairs to her attic bedroom. She sat up as the door opened.

'Good morning Molly,' said Molly's Mum. 'I have to go out this morning. Will you be alright getting breakfast for yourself and going to school without me?'

Molly nodded and rubbed grains of sleep out of the corners of her eyes. 'Where are you going?' she asked.

'I'm going to Stags Farm to see Lord and Lady Baxter, Joey's parents,' said Molly's Mum. 'One of their mares is trying to have a foal and they need my help. They telephoned five minutes ago and I need to get there quickly otherwise the foal and its Mum may die.'

Molly sat up straight. 'I'll be ok. Please hurry and save Joey's horses.'

Molly's Mum smiled. 'I'll be at the school gates to meet you this afternoon.' Then she turned on her heels and marched down the stairs. There was the faint rustle as she put on her all-weather jacket and the faint click of the front door closing.

Molly stood up and went to her front-facing bedroom window to wave goodbye to her Mum. She got dressed and brushed her hair and teeth. She fetched a bowl of cereal from the kitchen and brought it back to her bedroom where she perched on the windowsill, hoping Bob would visit.

To her delight, as she finished her cereal, Bob flew in like a rocket and landed with precision on the outside window ledge. He hopped inside and cocked his head towards Molly.

'I have some news,' said Bob. 'I know why the cats and dogs are being sick,' he added, puffing up his chest, the yellow feathers shimmering with his sense of importance.

'Oh Bob!' exclaimed Molly. 'That's marvellous. What's causing it? How did you find out?'

'Well,' started Bob, and Molly knew she needed to hurry her friend otherwise his tale would take an hour and she would be late for school.

'You'll have to tell me on the way to school,' said Molly. 'I'll get my coat and meet you outside the front door.'

Molly ushered Bob out of her bedroom and ran down

the stairs. She paused to deposit her empty cereal bowl and spoon into the dishwasher. She threw on her school jacket, picked up her rucksack, unlocked the front door and carefully locked it behind her.

She giggled as Bob landed on her shoulder. 'You're like a parrot,' she whispered to him.

'Humph!' said Bob. 'I think you'll find I'm better than a parrot.'

'Yes, of course you are,' laughed Molly. 'Now, please tell me, what's making the animals sick?'

'Well,' said Bob, and Molly groaned inside, this was going to be hard work to find out the reason.

She moved her jacket collar slightly to stop Bob's breath from tickling her ear.

'You have until we get to the school gates to tell me,' said Molly. 'Otherwise, it will have to wait until bedtime as I've got some friends coming round for tea.'

'Very well Molly Manila,' said Bob. 'I will be quick.'

Molly nodded. 'Very quick,' she muttered.

'If you don't want me to tell you just say so,' Bob sniffed. 'I don't like Sheba, so I don't care if she gets sick.'

'Oh Bob!' exclaimed Molly.

'She doesn't like me,' said Bob, 'and I don't like her.'

'But what is making her sick?' asked Molly. 'What is making Crusty and Crumbs sick? You like them, don't you?

They give you fur for your nest. If they get sick there won't be any more bedding for your family.'

Bob nodded and Molly giggled as his feathers tickled her ear again. They were nearly at the school gates and Molly knew Bob would fly away as soon as he saw her friends.

'What is making everyone sick?' asked Molly.

Bob leaned close to Molly's ear. 'Chip shop fat,' said Bob. 'It's coming out of Catch of the Day.'

Molly gasped. 'Casey and Jasmine's shop? That's not possible.'

'Yes,' chirped Bob. 'The chip shop fat is put outside in a large container and the container is leaking. I don't think it's the fat itself that's the problem. I think it's the container. The container is really old and smells funny.'

'I must tell Jasmine and Casey,' said Molly. 'They're coming to dinner tonight. Thank you Bob, I'll see you later.'

Molly flicked her hand up near her collar. Bob perched on Molly's wrist for a brief moment and then he flew back towards her house.

There was no time to tell Casey or Jasmine anything all morning. Miss Learner had set a surprise maths test that required all of Molly's brainpower working out the complex equations.

Joey was missing from class and Molly knew he would be waiting for news about the horse and foal. The copper bell rang for breaktime and Molly found Joey waiting in the corridor by the coat pegs.

Everyone flooded out of the classroom. Joey didn't stop and chat but took his football out of his rucksack and went outside to play with Casey, Jasmine, Ravi and Robbie.

After break they were so muddy Miss Learner sent them to the separate boys and girls changing rooms to clean up. There was no time to ask about the horses.

Molly knew her Mum would have delivered the foal safely, but she would have liked to hear from Joey what colour it was and what they had named it.

At lunchtime, Miss Learner asked Molly to stay inside for an appraisal, or as Molly discovered, it was an informal interview to check that she was making friends and enjoying her time at the school.

Molly found out Miss Learner had a cat that was being sick. She didn't mention her friend Bob, or what Bob thought the cause might be, but she learned Miss Learner's cat was male, four years old, black with white paws and called Abacus. Molly made a mental note to ask Sheba if she knew Abacus the next time she was visiting Mrs McGillam's house.

When the lunch bell rang all of Molly's friends came back into the classroom and settled down for the afternoon lessons. It looked as though it had been raining as everyone's hair and clothes were wet. Molly was glad she'd been inside, even if it had made her feel different, highlighting the fact that she was new.

Miss Learner had rotated the seating plan and Molly found herself sitting next to Abigale Learner, Miss Learner's daughter. Abigale had long brown hair and was quiet and studious. She had a great sense of humour and loved cats as much as Miss Learner.

It had been Abigale's idea to call their cat Abacus and she revealed to Molly that she would love another cat, or maybe two, or three. Molly suspected Abigale would have a house full of cats if her Mum let her. Molly also found out Abigale had a crush on Joey Baxter.

The lessons blurred from Maths to Geography to Language and then the end of school bell rang loudly above the school entrance.

'Homework in on Monday morning please,' said Miss Learner, her voice barely audible above the scraping of chairs on the floor as her students rushed to leave the room.

'If you do it this evening, you'll have the whole weekend free to do whatever you want,' continued Miss Learner. 'Remember, the school fete is coming up so you'll need to think about what you can bring to sell on your stalls.'

'What's the school fete?' Molly asked Abigale as they walked out of the classroom.

Abigale looked at Molly in surprise. 'I thought Mum would have told you all about it. We make cakes to sell and raise money for the school. We can also bring in old toys, games, clothes, anything we don't want anymore and people from the village come and buy them.'

'Oh,' said Molly. 'I went through all my things before we moved house. Everything I didn't want or didn't need went to an animal charity my Mum supports.'

'You could come round to my house and we could bake some cakes together, if you like?' said Abigale.

Molly nodded. 'I'd like that. I'm not very good at baking so you'll have to help me.'

Abigale laughed. 'Baking is easy. It's the icing that's tricky, especially if you want to do clever things like flowers or animal faces on top.'

'I'd like to try that,' said Molly. 'Oh, there's my Mum, I have to go.'

Abigale looked sad. 'My Mum likes to mark all the books before we go home, so I'm here for another hour usually.'

'Maybe we can go to your house and bake cakes next week after school? Would Miss Learner let us do that?'

'Maybe,' said Abigale, looking more cheerful. 'That would be great.'

'Hi Molly,' said Molly's Mum. She was standing at the school gates with a large packet of sweets in her hand. 'I've brought these for you, Casey and Jasmine to share,' she added, handing over the brightly coloured packet.

'Thank you Mrs Manila,' said Casey, taking the sweets and sharing them with Molly and his sister.

'Don't eat them all at once,' said Molly's Mum. 'I've got a special tea planned for the four of us.'

Molly took one of the squishy marshmallow sweets and popped it into her mouth.

'How did it go at Joey's farm?' Molly asked her Mum. 'Were the horses as beautiful as Joey says? Was the foal born safely? What colour was it? What's its name?'

'Questions, questions, questions!' Molly's Mum laughed and took one of the sweets. 'Joey has a magnificent new foal and lots and lots of land. There's a large stable for the horses, a coach house, a chapel, a lake and so much more I didn't get to see.'

'What about the foal?' asked Molly, her brown eyes bright with curiosity. 'Was it easy to deliver?'

'Eventually,' said Molly's Mum. 'It took a little strength to draw him out but he's going to be a fine horse. He has a lovely glossy black coat. Joey was there and he wants to call the foal Midnight.'

'Midnight,' repeated Molly. 'A black horse called Midnight.'

'Joey turned up late today,' said Casey. 'He never said

anything about a new horse.'

'Only because he's as mad on football as we are,' Jasmine laughed. 'Did you hear Dad's getting us tickets to the next Henley game?'

'Really?' said Casey. 'That'll be a great game!'

'We'll have to work for them,' said Jasmine. 'Just a few hours in the shop, but it will be worth it.'

'I've never been to a football match,' said Molly. 'Is it good?'

'It's the best,' said Jasmine. 'I want to play professionally when I'm older.'

'It's good to have ambitions,' said Molly's Mum as they reached the driveway at home. 'You'll probably need a sports scholarship.'

Jasmine nodded. 'I know. I'm working as much as I can to pay for coaching, kit and extra lessons.'

Molly's Mum opened the front door and let everyone inside.

'I need to check my answerphone and emails,' said Molly's Mum, letting herself into the surgery through the internal door. 'Play in the garden if you like and we'll have dinner at six 'o clock promptly.'

'Thank you Mrs Manila,' said Casey. He took out a black and white football from his rucksack. I know there's a big garden out the back as I used to come here when I was younger.'

Molly led the way through the lounge and out through the patio doors into the garden. She saw Bob perched by the flowerpots and remembered the acorn she had planted.

With a quick detour, she peeked into the terracotta pot. A tiny green fleck was growing in the flowerpot and Molly felt a pang of homesickness remembering the friends she had left behind.

'Come on Molly!' shouted Casey. 'What are you looking at?'

'Nothing!' shouted Molly. 'Just a tree I've planted,' she added under her breath.

At a quarter to six, Molly's Mum appeared at the patio door. She tapped her watch and called to them.

'Fifteen minutes until dinnertime,' said Molly's Mum. 'Come in and wash your hands please.'

Molly rolled her eyes. It never seemed necessary to go through all the rituals before dinner, especially in front of her friends and when they were having so much fun playing in the garden. After the football practice they had run all the way around the garden, climbed some of the trees and found a place to make a den.

In less than ten minutes later, they were sitting neatly at the dining table with the best knives and forks, the guest dinner plates and cloth napkins. Molly's Mum brought out a starter of toast soldiers with different flavours of chutney to dunk them in.

When the plates were empty, Molly helped clear the table and helped bring a magnificent roast chicken on a silver plate from the kitchen along with side dishes of roast potatoes, peas, carrots and a glass boat filled with thick brown gravy.

'I thought you might like a change from fish and chips,' said Molly's Mum. 'When I chatted with your Mum she said roast chicken was your favourite.'

'It is,' said Casey, licking his lips as he stared at the silver plate.

Molly enjoyed dinner with her friends. It was the weekend with no school for two whole days. Jasmine was telling her about the football training. Casey said he enjoyed playing but that he wasn't bothered about being picked to play for a team.

'Please will you clear the table Molly?' asked Molly's Mum. 'I've got some paperwork to finish from today. Jasmine, you and Casey are being picked up just after ten o'clock so there's plenty of time to play in the garden or watch TV.'

'That's when the shop shuts,' explained Jasmine. 'At the weekend we're allowed to stay up until midnight if we want.'

'Except you always fall asleep,' said Casey, poking his

sister in the ribs.

'Midnight, like Joey's horse,' said Molly, her imagination full of a small dark foal taking his first steps around the stable.

Jasmine and Casey helped Molly take all the dinner plates, cutlery and glasses into the kitchen. Casey loaded the dishwasher at great speed.

'I do it all the time in the shop,' he said, rolling the glasses over the back of his hand, flipping them in the air, catching them and placing them gently into the space on the dishwasher tray. 'I never break anything, well, nearly never,' he admitted, seeing Jasmine rolling her eyes at him.

'Shall we watch some TV?' asked Molly when all the dishes were loaded into the machine and the dishwasher beeped and started its cleaning cycle.

Jasmine and Casey looked at each other and then looked at Molly.

'There's football on,' said Jasmine. 'Is it ok to watch the game?'

Molly nodded. They were her guests and although she wouldn't normally have watched the football she thought it might be fun and she wanted to spend time with her new friends.

As the players walked out of the tunnel onto the pitch Molly found herself getting into the game. She tried to keep up as Jasmine talked non-stop over the commentators, agreeing and arguing with Casey in equal measure. Molly soon found out they supported different teams.

At half time, the adverts came on. One advert was for cat food and Molly remembered Sheba and what Bob had told her. She took a deep breath and turned the volume off on the TV.

'What did you do that for?' asked Jasmine. 'Aren't you enjoying the game?'

'I want to say something,' said Molly. 'Something important.'

'What is it?' asked Casey. 'Is everything ok?'

Molly nodded then shook her head. 'I think there's something wrong with the way you're disposing the chip fat at the shop,' said Molly, running the words together in one breath. 'I think the village cats and dogs are eating something from the container and it's making them sick.'

'Really?' asked Jasmine. 'That's awful!'

'No way,' said Casey. 'It's my job to empty the fryers. The fat goes into the container and the container gets emptied every Tuesday.'

'It's an old container,' said Jasmine. 'Maybe there's something wrong with it.'

'There's not,' said Casey. He scratched his head. 'Well maybe,' he paused looking at Jasmine and Molly both looking at him. 'When we get home we can have a look.'

'We'll have a look,' said Jasmine, 'and then we can let you know on Monday.'

Molly breathed a sigh of relief. It had gone better than she expected and she hoped Bob would be pleased. She turned the volume back up on the TV and the second half of the football started almost straightaway.

Jasmine kicked off her shoes and tucked her feet up on the sofa. Casey leaned forward and Molly fetched glasses of lemonade and some salt and vinegar crisps to share. She passed around the plastic bowl and they ate with their eyes glued to the football players on the screen.

Molly's Mum joined them for the last ten minutes. Jasmine's team was winning and she was bouncing up and down on the sofa urging the players to hold on until the end. The referee blew his whistle and she leaped up from the sofa punching her fist into the air.

'We've won!' shouted Jasmine.

'Again,' grumbled Casey.'

'So, change teams,' said Jasmine. She yawned loudly. 'Is it nearly ten o'clock yet?'

Molly's Mum nodded and collected the empty bowl and glasses. Just as she returned from the kitchen the doorbell rang and Mr and Mrs Cooper were standing at the front door. They had arrived in their mobile fish and chip van. Mr

Cooper game Molly's Mum a parcel of fish and instructions to re-heat it in the oven tomorrow.

'Remember to have a look at the container,' said Molly as Jasmine and Casey put on their shoes and coats, collected their school rucksacks and with a flurry of activity, they were gone.

'Did you enjoy having your friends around tonight?' asked Molly's Mum as she and Molly cleared away the dinner dishes. 'I've got to go to Joey's farm on Monday and Lady Baxter has said you can come with me if you like.

'Yes please!' said Molly. 'I really want to meet Midnight and see Joey's house. It sounds amazing there!'

'That's good,' said Molly's Mum. 'They want me there for most of the day and I didn't like to have you coming home from school on your own especially if I need to work on into the evening. I'll finish clearing up if you want to go to bed.'

'I'll help,' said Molly. 'Did you get all your paperwork done?'

Molly's Mum nodded. 'I did, and I had a phone call from your Dad. He sends you his love.'

Molly smiled. That's what her Mum always told her. She was rarely allowed to speak to him while he was away and she was really looking forward to when he would be back for a few weeks. She helped unload the dishwasher and packed the glasses, cutlery and dishes neatly away.

When the last dish was safely in the cupboard Molly went upstairs to brush her hair and her teeth and got changed into her pyjamas. Molly's Mum came into her room and kissed her goodnight.

Five minutes after Molly's Mum had gone downstairs to her bedroom Bob tapped on Molly's window and hopped inside.

'Hello Molly Manila,' said Bob. He hopped from foot to foot and stared at the empty saucer. 'Did you forget me tonight?'

'Yes,' confessed Molly. 'But don't worry, I've got a packet of nuts and seeds under my bed.'

She got out of bed and fished around her pairs of shoes under her bed for the birdseed packet. Her hands closed around the large sack of food and she took it over to Bob.

'I've told Jasmine and Casey about the problem with the container at their fish and chip shop,' said Molly, carefully pouring two handfuls of nuts and seeds into Bob's saucer.

'And?' said Bob. He bent his neck to pick up a seed in his beak. 'Will they do anything about it?' his voice grew muffled as he noisily hoovered up most of the nuts and seeds in the saucer.

'I think so,' said Molly, covering her mouth with her hand as she yawned. It was only half past ten but she was

74

quite tired. 'They'll tell me at school on Monday.'

'Very good Molly Manila,' said Bob. 'Sleep well,' he added and with a whir of wings he flew out of the open window.

7

STAGS FARM

On Monday morning sunlight streamed through Molly Manila's bedroom window waking her out of a deep sleep and a dream about black horses galloping through the open fields. She lifted her arm to tap her alarm clock and realised it wasn't chiming. She had woken up almost an hour before she needed to get ready for school.

Not wanting to waste the morning, Molly checked she had all her schoolbooks packed into her rucksack. She sharpened her pencils and swept the shavings into her wastepaper bin. A tap on her window made her look up. Bob was there, tipping his head to look sideways at her.

'You're up early,' said Bob, hopping inside the open window.

'I am,' agreed Molly. 'The sunlight woke me up.'

'Me too,' said Bob, opening his beak as if to yawn. 'Have you got any more sunflower seeds? I'm rather hungry this morning.'

'You're always hungry,' said Molly, tucking her freshly sharpened pencils into the side pocket of her rucksack. 'I'll get you some seeds.'

Molly fetched the sack from under her bed and scattered a handful of sunflower seeds into the saucer. She watched as Bob helped himself, plucking the seeds to open them.

'Thank you, Molly Manila,' said Bob. He clasped two sunflower seeds in his clawed foot and spread his wings. 'Have a nice day at school. You'll be late home today so make sure you pack some snacks.'

'Late home?' said Molly. 'Why will I be late home?' She stuck her hands on her hips as Bob winked at her and took off. 'I know I need to make sure the problem at the fish and chip shop is sorted,' Molly said to herself, 'but perhaps Bob knows something I don't.'

Molly filled up the saucer with more seeds and got back into bed. She sat up reading a few chapters of her favourite book. It was about a boy who had a dragon egg and it was very exciting.

Before long, Molly's alarm clock began to jiggle on her bedside table and began a happy chiming, announcing it was time to get up properly.

Molly threw back her duvet, got dressed and ate breakfast in the kitchen with her Mum.

'Remember we're going to Stags Farm today,' said Molly's Mum. 'I'll be there all day and I've arranged with Lady Baxter that you will meet me at their house with Joey after school.'

'Will I get to go in the Rolls Royce?' asked Molly, her eyes widening.

'It's just a car,' said Molly's Mum. 'A big car, but still a car.'

Molly grinned. Her Mum wasn't easily impressed by other people's money. Molly was sure Lord and Lady Baxter would have many members of staff to look after their farm and everything on it.

'I'll drive you to school today and then I can go straight to Stags Farm,' said Molly's Mum. 'You can have an extra few minutes at home to tidy your room. I keep seeing a saucer on your windowsill. If you insist on feeding birds in your bedroom then you must tidy up afterwards. I don't want rats running around the house.'

Molly skipped up to her room giving this some thought. If she remembered she would ask Bob later whether there were any rats in the village.

It was unlikely, she thought, considering the number of cats patrolling the village. She thought of Sheba and wondered if Mrs McGillam's Siamese cat had made a full recovery.

Molly tidied up the seed husks Bob had scattered and swept them into her wastepaper bin. Thinking about her Mum's warning about rats, she picked up the bin and took it downstairs, emptying the contents into the kitchen bin.

With a few skips Molly took the bin back upstairs, had a quick look out of the window to see if she could see any sign of Bob, and skipped back downstairs again.

It felt silly driving the hundred yards to the school gates but Molly jumped in the car and jumped out again as they arrived. She kissed her Mum on the cheek, shut the car door and waved as her Mum drove off. She checked both directions, crossed the road and found she was the first to arrive in the playground.

Molly walked around the play equipment, swinging on the bars and climbing to the top of the wooden tower.

From the top of the tower, Molly could see Casey and Jasmine walking together from the village square. They were taking it in turns to kick a black and white football attached to a rope. From the other direction, Molly could see Abigale and Miss Learner walking towards the school. Abigale stopped to stroke a cat that crossed her path.

A soft mechanical purring made Molly turn her head and she saw Joey Baxter arriving at school in his parents silver

Rolls Royce. Mr Tomkins stopped the car beside the school gates. He stepped out of the driver's side and opened the passenger door for Joey.

With gentlemanly poise, Joey stepped gracefully out of the car and stood up straight. He walked slowly to the school gate, then ran into the playground as soon as Mr Tomkins had driven away. Joey threw down his schoolbag and leapt up the wooden tower to join Molly.

'You're early,' said Joey.

Molly nodded. 'Mum dropped me off. She's going to your house to look at the horses this morning.'

'She's spending the whole day at ours,' said Joey, his eyes gleaming, 'and you're coming to dinner.'

'I know,' said Molly, grinning at Joey, 'and I know you've got a new foal called Midnight as well.'

Joey nodded. 'It's my foal. I have to look after her and I'll be able to ride her and enter competitions when I'm older.'

'Don't you have staff for that?' asked Molly. 'I thought you'd have stable boys and girls to muck out the stables and look after your horses?'

'We do,' said Joey, 'and lots of people use our stables. I can't wait to show you. Some of them are thoroughbred racehorses worth millions of pounds!'

Molly grinned. Joey made it all sound so normal, but it

was beyond her wildest dreams to live among so many animals. She thought of Archie the hedgehog she hadn't seen for a few weeks and Bob who told her there were many animals in her garden. She made up her mind to find as many as she could at the weekend.

Jasmine and Casey were next to arrive. Molly swung herself down from the wooden tower and Joey leapt from the top, landing sure-footed on the bark chippings.

'It's only a bit higher than jumping off a horse,' said Joey, laughing at Molly's shocked face. 'You'll see later.'

Molly nodded but secretly she wasn't sure she would ever be brave enough to jump off a fully grown horse.

Casey removed the rope from the football and started kicking the ball to Jasmine and Joey. Ravi and Robbie arrived next, followed by Miss Learner and Abigale.

Miss Learner unlocked the school doors to let everyone in early. Molly put her coat on her peg and joined her friends in the classroom. She sat next to Joey. Abigale sat on his other side and they chatted about horses, cats, dogs and sheep while Miss Learner wrote notes about the Kings and Queens of England on the whiteboard and played a short video to help them learn the names and dates.

After lunch was Sports. Mr Wicket, their very tall and thin, ex-professional cricket player, sports teacher took the lesson. He towered above the children, his blond fringe flopping in his blue eyes and he was wearing his usual navy tracksuit with white stripes down the legs and a sparkling white tshirt

Mr Wicket arrived armed with coloured bibs and orange cones. He waved to Miss Learner through the classroom window and within the first few minutes he had set up a rigorous course designed to test their speed and agility.

He enthusiastically demonstrated the moves he wanted everyone to perform and then set time limits for each section.

Molly was exhausted when Mr Wicket finally blew his whistle and the lesson ended. There was just enough time to get changed back into school uniform from shorts and tshirts as the end of school bell rang loudly.

Joey held up Molly's coat from the row of pegs. 'You're coming round to ours tonight,' he reminded Molly.

Secretly, Molly had been looking forward to visiting Joey's home at Stags Farm all day. She was desperate to see the stables he had described and to see the new foal called Midnight her Mum had helped to deliver. She was also looking forward to meeting Lord and Lady Baxter and riding in the silver Rolls Royce with Mr Tomkins.

Molly put her arms into the coat sleeves and pulled her jacket on. She zipped it up even though it wasn't cold and slung her rucksack over her shoulder.

'Let's go!' said Joey and he looked really excited to be showing Molly his house and the animals.

Mr Tomkins was waiting at the school gates. He was smartly dressed as usual in his black suit, crisp white shirt and an emerald tie dropping from his neck to his waist. He opened the back door behind his driver's seat and helped Molly inside. Then he went to the other side and opened the opposite door for Joey.

'Thank you,' said Molly. She liked the way she was sinking into the comfy leather seats. She fastened her seatbelt and barely noticed as the car purred away from the school. The engine was extremely quiet, unlike her Mum's car or the vans her Dad used for his work.

She listened as Mr Tomkins chatted about what had happened on the estate during the day and asked questions about their day at school. It felt rather formal but also very similar to her conversations with her Mum after school and Molly could tell Mr Tomkins was genuinely interested in what she and Joey were telling him.

Just outside of the village, Mr Tomkins took a turning up a lane marked "Private" and Molly noticed a grey stone wall appeared in the view from her window. Tall trees peeked over the top of the wall.

The wall ran for quite some time, then there was a gap and Molly saw two large stone stags standing on pillars with black wrought iron gates open and welcoming them into the estate.

There was a bump, bump, bump, as they drove over a cattlegrid and off the tarmac road onto a long, straight, smooth pale cream gravel driveway that led to a circular ring, like a mini roundabout, outside the biggest house Molly had ever seen.

The house was a tall, pale cream square with an arched roof covered in grey slate. There was a large porch with a triangle of marble supported by two marble pillars. Another stag, painted white and surrounded by four gold stars, was on a metal shield attached to the marble triangle.

Windows with white slatted wooden shutters were dotted irregularly from top to bottom. Molly counted five floors, plus windows at the top which were set into the slate roof. There were several brick chimneys at the far end of the building and small grey wisps of smoke spiralling out of ceramic chimney pots.

Dark green stems of ivy wound their way up the side of the house and around some of the windows. As they drove closer, Molly saw there were roses full of pink and red flowers growing in terracotta pots outside the front porch.

'This is my house,' Joey announced as Mr Tomkins stopped the Rolls Royce outside the front door.

Molly nodded. She couldn't find any words just yet.

'Do you like it?' asked Joey. 'What's up? Is something wrong?'

'No, nothing,' said Molly, tripping over her words. 'It's just, well, it's enormous!'

Joey laughed. 'Wait until you see the rest of it! We've got the stables around the back, a tennis court, swimming pool, sauna and everything!'

'And everything,' said Molly, unstrapping her seatbelt and shuffling to get out of the car as Mr Tomkins opened the door for her.

Molly took his hand and stepped down onto the cream coloured gravel, her school shoes crunching on the ground as she steadied herself. She reached for her rucksack and Mr Tomkins gently held back her arm.

'I'll see to that Miss Molly,' said Mr Tomkins. 'You go inside with Master Joey and meet Lord and Lady Baxter.'

Molly nodded, her mouth suddenly dry with nerves.

'Thank you Mr Tomkins,' said Joey. He took Molly's hand and marched up the two marble steps into the porchway. 'Welcome to Stags Farm!'

'It's bigger than I was expecting,' whispered Molly as they entered the flagstone floored hallway. 'When you said it was called "Stags Farm" I thought it would be a farmhouse not a country mansion!'

Joey shrugged. 'It's just my home. I bet it's not that

different from yours.'

Molly shook her head. Joey lived in another world. She followed him at a quick pace as they passed doorway after doorway. They turned a corner and Molly was suddenly blinded by daylight as they passed a grand dining room with a conservatory style glass roof and walls. Joey hurried her on and opened a large arched doorway.

'Hello Mummy,' said Joey. 'This is Molly Manilla, my friend from school,' he introduced Molly to a kind looking woman sitting in a plush red armchair with gold tassels.

Molly stared at the enormous room. It seemed to be a large lounge with family portraits lined on all the walls from floor to ceiling. A large fireplace was at the far end with a marble mantlepiece filled with purple candles in tall silver candlestick holders. Above the fireplace was the familiar Baxter family shield, the white stag and four gold stars.

The woman stood up and Molly could see it was Lady Baxter straightaway. She had the same light brown hair as Joey and the same bright blue eyes. She wore a red riding jacket with a white polo neck jumper tucked into the waist of navy denim jeans and black knee-high leather boots. A string of large marble sized pearls was around her neck dropping halfway to her waist. They matched two marble sized pearl earrings and her dazzling white smile as she greeted Joey and Molly.

'Hello Molly Manila,' said Lady Baxter. 'Welcome to our home. Would you like a drink while you wait for your Mum to finish looking at the horses?'

Molly opened her mouth, about to say yes please to the drink, when Joey nudged her.

'Molly would like to see the horses,' said Joey, winking at Molly. 'May we go to the stables first?'

Laughter lines appeared in the corners of Lady Baxter's eyes. 'Is that what Molly Manila wishes Joey, or is that what you'd like her to do first?'

Joey grinned sheepishly. 'Both,' he said, raising his eyebrows as though it was never in question what they would do first.

'Very well,' said Lady Baxter, sitting back down in her chair. 'I have a telephone call to make and then tea will be at five o'clock followed by dinner at seven thirty.'

Joey led Molly out of the lounge, down another long corridor and out of a side door. The door led out into a walled garden filled with flowers. Molly noticed all the flowers were pink and red roses and wondered if they were Lady Baxter's favourite flowers.

Beyond the walled garden was an enormous grass lawn leading as far as the eye could see. Far away in the distance were trees and bushes, but they were so small from where Molly was standing.

'These are the stables,' said Joey, pulling at Molly's sleeve. He pointed at a horseshoe shaped grey stone single storey building with a thatched roof.

The building was divided into stalls for the horses. There were many wooden stable doors, with the top half of each door pinned back against the wall and the bottom half of the door closed.

Over the top of some of the half-closed doors Molly could see horses peering out to see who was coming into their cobbled courtyard. There were brown horses, grey horses, white horses and at the far end, Molly could see her Mum's veterinary bag perched on the floor beside one of the half open doors. She noticed beside each door was a wooden plaque with different names carved into the wood and coloured in with black paint.

'That's Midnight's stall,' said Joey, pointing to the stall Molly was looking at. 'Your Mum's probably in there.'

Molly nodded. 'She might not want to be disturbed if she's working. We could say hello and then you could show me the other horses.'

Joey nodded. 'Hi Mrs Manila, we're back from school,' he called through the open hatch.

Moments later there was a rustle and Molly's Mum appeared at the doorway. Molly hardly recognised her Mum. She was wearing a white plastic coat over her trousers and shirt. The coat was stained in places with dark brown streaks and pieces of straw were hanging from the seams.

'Hello Joey, hello Molly,' said Molly's Mum. 'I'm nearly finished here with Midnight. He's going to be a fine horse. I've just got to check Daisy, Dewdrop and Alaska and then I can join you.'

Molly peered into the stable. She could see a large brown horse and the tiny black foal nestled together. Molly guessed the large brown horse was Midnight's Mum. She could have found out by asking but it looked like they wanted to be left alone. This was confirmed when the large brown horse turned to Molly and opened her mouth, revealing two rows of large square teeth.

Molly took a step backwards, then leaned closer as she realised the horse was talking to her.

'Horse thieves are coming,' said the large brown horse. 'Don't let them take Midnight.'

Molly gasped and put her hand quickly over her mouth. 'Horse thieves?' she whispered.

Molly's Mum looked at Molly and laughed. 'I don't think horse thieves would be able to get into Stags Farm, do you?'

Molly shrugged. She knew what she'd heard. Some of the horses in the stables must be worth a hundred thousand pounds or more.

Joe pointed at the stable doors opposite Midnight's stall.

'They belong to my sister and her friends,' he said dismissively. 'They only ride them at the weekends. Now I've got my own horse I'll be riding him every day, as soon as I'm allowed to ride him. I muck out most of the stables myself and all the horses love me,' he added.

Molly agreed as Joey rubbed the nose of each horse they passed. Each horse nuzzled against his hand and their heads turned to follow him as he moved on from stall to stall.

She counted sixteen stalls and sixteen horses coming up to the half open doors to greet them as they walked past. She could see how it would be a big job for her Mum to look after the horses' health as well as the other animals at the farm she had yet to meet.

'Ooo!' squeaked Molly as a large white goose came running up behind her.

Joey doubled up with laughter. 'This is Dozy,' he said, bending down and stroking the goose's head.

With a quiet grunt the goose wound her neck around Joey's forearm affectionately.

'She's supposed to be with the ducks out on the pond,' said Joey. 'I'll show you the pond. It's really good.'

He picked up the goose in both arms and cradled it like a baby. The goose rested her head on Joey's shoulder and allowed him to walk down the grass lawn away from the stables and towards an enormous expanse of water complete with a jetty and a boathouse.

'This is the pond,' said Joey. 'Well, actually it's more like a lake or nature reserve. We've got geese, ducks, water voles and loads of frogs.' He set Dozy down on the bank and she sat watching as five ducks landed gracefully in the middle of the water.

Molly grinned. Joey was playing down the size of his house and everything it contained. She spied two small rowing boats inside the boathouse and imagined what it would be like to row gently across the lake surrounded by friendly ducks bobbing on the surface.

Joey checked his watch. 'It's nearly five o'clock,' he said, a worried look on his face. 'Mummy doesn't like me to be late for tea. She's got changed since this morning and that means she's been baking. I hope you like cake,' he grinned.

The next thing Molly knew was being dragged by her hand and running back across the long lawn, through the kitchen garden and back into the lounge exactly as the grandfather clock in the hallway vibrated on the stone floor and chimed five long tuneful melodies.

'Haven't got time to wash our hands,' said Joey. He took a deep breath and opened the lounge door.

Inside the lounge, Mr Tomkins was serving small glasses of elderflower cordial in crystal glasses to the adults. He began with Lady Baxter and she took a sip and nodded her approval.

Mr Tomkins moved on to Molly's Mum, who had taken off her white plastic veterinary coat and was wearing a cotton dress with sunflowers on, and he served her a glass of elderflower cordial. Mr Tomkins then served Lord Baxter, who was wearing blue denim jeans and a blue and black chequered shirt.

Molly was surprised. She had half expected Lord Baxter to be wearing a tuxedo or a dinner suit. Perhaps he would change for dinner which it seemed was being served at seven thirty.

Mr Tomkins returned to the drinks table and served Molly and Joey the same elderflower cordial but in thicker, glass tumblers. He left the room and moments later a young woman entered the room. She was wearing a white apron over a beige skirt and black polo neck top. She carried a silver tray with a brightly coloured assortment of sponge cakes in different shapes and sizes.

'Hello,' she said. 'Today we have carrot cake, chocolate and beetroot cake and Victoria sponge with jam made from fruit from the garden. Everything has been made by Lady Baxter,' she added.

'I enjoy baking,' said Lady Baxter in a rather posh voice. 'I believe it is important to do as one wishes, regardless of one's position. I am privileged to be Lady of Stags Farm and

I am grateful to employ many staff here, but I still wish to bake cakes and spend time with my children and their friends.'

Molly took a slice of the chocolate and beetroot cake. She hadn't tried it before, nor if she was honest, even heard of the combination. She took a small bite and found it to be sticky and sweet with a definite hint of the beetroot coming through. She wondered for a moment whether it counted as a healthy food as it contained the vegetable, but decided it was too sweet to be any good for her.

'How was school, Joey?' asked Lord Baxter. 'Are they putting in a football team to play Henley City next month?'

'Mr Wicket hasn't told us yet,' said Joey. 'I expect we'll play them soon.'

Lord Baxter nodded. 'Let Mummy and I know when it's on and we'll come and watch.'

'That was lovely cake,' said Molly's Mum. Molly nodded her agreement.

'Do you bake, Maria?' asked Lady Baxter.

'Sometimes,' said Molly's Mum. 'We cook nearly every day and perhaps bake once a week, or for special occasions.'

When all of the slices of cake had been eaten, Joey asked if he could show Molly around the house while waiting for dinner.

Molly's Mum put on her white coat and said she would

check on the horses one last time. Molly noticed instead of wellies, her Mum was wearing a pair of cream slippers. They must have been borrowed as Molly didn't recognise them. For a brief moment, Molly had a fleeting imagination of what her Mum would look like wearing cream slippers outside in the dusty stable courtyard.

It didn't seem any time at all before Mr Tomkins returned to the sitting room and announced that dinner was ready.

Molly followed Joey and her Mum with Lord and Lady Baxter into a rather grand dining room. There was an enormously long dining table with enough chairs to seat twenty people. The table was lengthways in the middle of the room with a fireplace at one end and a sideboard against the wall at the other end.

The table was covered with a sparkling white tablecloth with four silver candlesticks placed at regular intervals. Silver cutlery was laid out in five places at the far end of the table. Molly noticed there seemed to be far more knives and forks than they would ever use at home.

'You're here Molly, sitting next to me' said Joey. 'Mrs Manila, would you like to sit opposite us?'

Molly noticed Joey had suddenly become very formal and efficient. His voice had dropped an octave and his face was serious. She wondered what sort of people usually sat at the table. Perhaps celebrities, TV stars, other Lords and Ladies, maybe even Royalty.

Just as Molly fantasied about sitting next to a princess the dining room door opened and Mr Tomkins arrived looking rather flustered.

'Just one moment,' said Mr Tomkins, bustling in the sideboard drawers. He swept up to the table and deftly put another complicated set of knives and forks down next to Molly. 'Lady Arabella is here.'

'Who?' asked Molly.

'My sister,' said Joey, a scowl overpowering his serious face. 'She's not supposed to be home until next weekend.'

'Problems with her accommodation,' said Mr Tomkins.

'Did she break up with her boyfriend?' asked Joey.

Mr Tomkins winked at Joey. 'Problems with her accommodation,' he repeated, 'and I won't hear of anything different.'

Joey nodded. Molly guessed this must happen a lot. She wondered what Lady Arabella might be like and she didn't have to wait long as the dining room door was flung violently open and a tall woman wearing black drainpipe trousers and a pink roll neck jumper marched into the room.

Lady Arabella was the exact image of Joey's Mum, Lady Baxter, with the same colour hair and upright walk.

'Hi Joey,' said Lady Arabella and she scooped Joey up

into a hug that lifted him off his feet.

'Put me down,' grumbled Joey, swinging his feet trying to kick her knees. 'I'm too old for that.'

'Embarrassing you in front of your girlfriend?' teased Lady Arabella. 'Hello, I'm Arabella, Joey's sister.'

'Pleased to meet you,' said Molly, holding out her hand, which was shook firmly and then released.

Lady Arabella sat at the table and folded her hands on top of the serviette. She tapped the table with her painted fingernails. Joey drew back the chair next to her and offered the place to Molly. He waited while she sat and then sat himself beside her.

'How are the horses?' asked Lady Arabella. 'I saw a Vet's van here. Is everything ok?'

'The horses are fine,' said Joey. 'I've got my own horse now. He's called Midnight.'

'My Mum is a Vet,' added Molly. 'She's here checking on the animals and updating their records.'

Lady Arabella nodded. 'We have a lot of animals. I'm going to spend the day riding tomorrow. Would you like to come?' she added, almost as an afterthought. 'Do you ride?'

Molly nodded. In her old town, she had riding lessons for an hour every Saturday.

'We've got school tomorrow,' said Joey. 'What are you doing here?'

'I'm moving back for a few weeks. Just until I find a new job and somewhere to live.' Lady Arabella smiled.

'Someone to live with,' muttered Joey.

'Maybe,' said Lady Arabella. 'Not that it's any of your business. I'm eighteen. I can do what I like.'

Molly leaned back as Joey was about to say something to his sister. She was glad when the door opened and Lord and Lady Baxter came into the room followed by her Mum.

They were followed by the young woman from earlier who opened a secret hatch in the wall beside the fireplace and started unloading plates of steaming vegetables which she set in front of everyone on the white tablecloth.

She returned to the hatch and, using both hands, she carried a large white ceramic dish that she set carefully next to Lord Baxter. She lifted the lid and Molly gasped. Inside was a pheasant.

'Are we eating that?' Molly asked, regretting the words as soon as they were spoken.

Lord Baxter looked up in surprise. Her Mum looked sternly at her. Lady Arabella let out a giggle.

'We always have pheasant on Thursdays,' said Lord Baxter, as though this was perfectly normal. 'Are you a vegetarian?'

Molly shook her head. 'I'm sorry. I wasn't expecting to see…' she faltered, looking at the eyes of the dead bird. She wondered whether it had been bred for eating or shot for sport.

Lord Baxter picked up a large carving knife and sliced slithers of meat, serving them to Molly's Mum, Molly, Lady Baxter, Arabella, Joey and finally heaping several thick slices onto his own plate.

Molly saw while Lord Baxter had been serving the meat, the woman waitressing for them had returned several times with various coloured sauces and glasses of wine and more elderflower cordial. She brought a thick gravy in a long boat shaped jug. She checked everyone had everything they wanted and left the family, Molly and her Mum to eat their meal.

Outside it was getting dark and as the plates were cleared away Molly's Mum announced they would be heading home. Lady Baxter fetched their coats and Molly's rucksack from school.

Molly got into the passenger side of her Mum's car. Joey came up and tapped on the window. Molly wound the window down halfway.

'Thank you for coming round,' said Joey. 'I wanted you to be the first person to see Midnight.'

Molly nodded. She had a funny feeling in her stomach. When they had been in the stables earlier, Midnight's Mum had whispered to her. Something about horse thieves.

Something about someone wanting a black horse.

'Joey, make sure you lock Midnight's stall tightly tonight,' said Molly, looking intently at Joey. 'Make sure no one can get into the stables.'

Joey looked quizzically at Molly and nodded. 'I'll do it myself,' he said.

Mr Tomkins opened the car door for Molly's Mum and closed it behind her. 'Safe journey,' said Mr Tomkins, stepping back as Molly's Mum turned the ignition and the engine fired into life.

Molly fastened her seatbelt as they drove off, the wheels spinning on the gravel, then the journey was smooth as they drove down the concrete drive and back onto the lane that joined the main road back into the village.

As Molly's Mum parked, Molly noticed some lights were on in the house.

'Your Dad is home,' said Molly's Mum. 'He has a couple of days off and wanted to surprise you by coming home for the weekend.'

Molly beamed. She had missed her Dad and wanted to tell him all about Joey and Midnight. The front door opened and her Dad's familiar silhouette appeared. Molly rushed forward and was scooped up into a bear hug.

Molly was swung round and round until she was a little bit dizzy. Then her feet touched the floor and they were heading into the lounge via the kitchen, collecting snacks and listening to her Dad talking about his days on the road and her Mum talking about life in the village and the visit to Stags Farm.

When it was possible to get a word in edgeways, Molly talked non-stop about Stags Farm, Joey, Midnight, the delicious cakes and pheasant for dinner. Her Dad took in all the details and smiled.

'Sounds like Joey has a thing for you,' he said, grinning.

'No way!' laughed Molly. 'Abigale at school likes Joey.'

'But does he like her?' teased her Dad. 'Did she get to go round to his house?'

'I only went because Mum was seeing their animals,' said Molly indignantly, her cheeks flushing. 'I don't like him like that!'

'Good,' said her Dad. 'At least I won't need to have a word with him,' he added, the corners of his mouth creasing with laughter.

Molly's parents finished the crisps and bottle of wine. Molly found she was nearly asleep and she remembered she had to be up early for school the next day.

'Bedtime Molly,' said her Dad. 'I'll still be here in the morning. We've got the whole weekend together.'

Molly smiled and gave both her parents a hug. She danced out of the room and upstairs. She stopped in the bathroom to clean her teeth and change into her pyjamas.

She folded her clothes and stacked them in her wardrobe ready for the morning. She checked her alarm clock was set and went over to the windowsill with a handful of birdseeds for Bob.

With a whirring of wings, Bob appeared. 'I wondered what time you were coming to bed tonight,' Bob scolded. 'Just because your Dad is home, it doesn't mean you can stay up late.'

'You're just grumpy because I'm late feeding you,' said Molly, tidying up after Bob as he scattered the seeds out of the saucer onto the windowsill.

'How was Stags Farm?' asked Bob. 'Was it as you expected?'

Molly nodded, hiding a yawn behind her hand. 'It was really good,' she said, then thinking about Midnight, she added, 'but one of the horses told me there might be horse thieves coming.'

Bob cocked his head to one side. 'Horse thieves?' he asked. 'I'll fly there tonight and see if I can see anything.'

'Thank you Bob,' said Molly, yawning again. She left the saucer on the windowsill and the window slightly ajar.

She was aware of Bob watching her as she got under her duvet. Her dark hair spanned out on the pillow and Molly just managed to call out goodnight before she fell asleep.

8

BOB HAS THE ANSWER

Molly woke abruptly the following morning. There was a chirping in her ear and a whirring of wings brushing her face. She swatted her arms around, gradually adjusting to what was happening.

Bob was circling inches above her face, his tiny wings fluttering anxiously, his little bird voice high pitched and agitated.

'Molly Manila you must wake up,' said Bob. 'Wake up!'

Molly raised herself up using her elbows. 'What is it Bob?'

'Horse thieves,' said Bob, landing on Molly's arm.

Molly flinched. It was the first time Bob had touched her and she felt honoured. She lifted her arm closer to her face so she could try and understand her friend's gibbering chirps. She gradually understood.

Last night after leaving her house, Bob had visited Stags Farm and landed on the stable roof above Midnight's stall. He had planned to keep watch for an hour and then return just before dawn.

'And they came,' said Bob, running his words together. 'There were four of them. Two men and two women. All wearing riding jodhpurs and long coats with brass buttons. They opened the stall and took Midnight. I watched as they led him out of the stable and into the field. They set him free to run around the field and into the woods.'

Molly put her hand over her mouth. Joey would be devastated. 'What happened next?' she asked, hardly daring to speak.

'After a few minutes, one of them put reins around Midnight and led him back into the stall,' said Bob, his tiny bird breaths coming thick and fast. 'And one of them was Lady Arabella,' he finished, tipping his head sideways and staring at Molly with one very black beady eye.

'Oh,' said Molly. 'Lady Arabella is Joey's sister. I wonder what she was doing.'

'Showing off maybe,' suggested Bob, hopping from foot to foot and tickling Molly's forearm. 'Maybe she was going to set Midnight free and couldn't go through with it.'

'Maybe,' said Molly thoughtfully. 'I can ask Joey about it at school today. He was supposed to lock the stable door. I'll ask him why he didn't.'

Bob nodded. 'How will you explain that you know?' he asked gently. 'He won't believe you if you tell him I've told you what happened.'

'I'll have to ask him carefully,' said Molly. 'Maybe I can ask if he heard anything unusual, or if he knows if Lady Arabella went out last night.'

'There must be a reason for it,' said Bob. 'If Lady Arabella hasn't got any money perhaps she wanted to sell Midnight and then she could afford to live somewhere else.'

Molly gasped. 'She wouldn't do that, would she?'

'I don't know,' said Bob. 'They're a funny family.'

'I'll ask Joey at school today,' said Molly, throwing back the duvet and getting out of bed. She opened her curtains and found her school uniform to wear. As she fastened her shoes Bob flew onto her shoulder.

'Be careful,' chirped Bob and then he was flying out of the window and down the garden.

'Be careful?' asked Molly. 'What do you mean be careful?' but her question went unanswered and she skipped down the stairs to have breakfast with her parents.

Joey wasn't at the school gates when Molly arrived at school. There was no silver Rolls Royce pulling up to the school even when the school bell sounded. Molly stared up the road. There was no sign of Joey at all this morning.

Molly went into the classroom with Jasmine and Casey. Jasmine was talking non-stop about football and how she was going for try-outs at a bigger team than the one run by the school.

'We haven't heard from Joey,' said Casey. 'Didn't you go round his house yesterday? Don't you know where he is?'

Molly was suddenly aware Abigale was listening to their conversation.

'I only went round there because my Mum is looking after all of the animals at Stags Farm,' said Molly.

Abigale breathed a deep sigh and walked off.

They sat in their usual seats in class. Molly was by the window, looking out for Bob, even though she didn't expect him to check on her, it was nice knowing he was around.

As Molly took out her paper and pencil, she overheard her classmates Robbie and Ravi. She heard the words "Stags" and "Midnight" and was instantly alert. Without making it obvious, Molly leaned back in her chair to hear more.

'So it was stolen?' asked Ravi.

'Last night,' said Robbie. 'Dad says it was horse thieves. He'll find out who did it.'

'Who did what?' demanded Molly, spinning round in her chair, all pretence of not listening evaporating as she wanted to know what had happened.

'Joey's horse,' said Robbie. 'Midnight has been stolen. That's why Joey isn't here today. My Dad's gone to his house to take statements and ask lots of questions,' he added importantly, 'so the Police can hunt down who's done this.'

Molly clasped her hand over her mouth. Poor Joey. No wonder he wasn't in school today. Even though he'd only had the foal a few days Midnight meant everything to Joey.

'Turn to page twenty three,' said Miss Learner and Molly found her hands were shaking as she opened her text book.

She could hardly concentrate and Miss Learner kept Molly back as she dismissed the class for breaktime.

'Are you worried about Joey?' asked Miss Learner, her brown eyes looking kindly at Molly.

Molly nodded with tears in her eyes. 'Midnight is just a baby horse,' she said. 'How could someone do that?'

'Sergeant Stopper will find out who's done this,' Miss Learner tried to reassure Molly. 'He is the very best policeman in the village,' she added, smiling into the distance.

'He's the only policeman in the village,' said Molly.

Miss Learner nodded. 'And a very good policeman too.'

Molly edged away from Miss Learner. 'Please may I go now?' she asked.

'Of course,' said Miss Learner. 'Try and take your mind off things.'

Molly tried her best but the rest of the day passed in a blur. She was glad to see her Dad at the school gates. It was rare for him to meet her and she ran up to him, hugging him tightly and telling him all about Midnight on their walk back up the road towards home.

'So, this Sergeant Stopper,' said Molly's Dad. 'Is he good at his job?'

Molly nodded. 'I think so,' she said, thinking back to some of the stories Robbie had told about his Dad, all the crimes he had solved in the village. Even allowing for Robbie to exaggerate a little, his Dad did seem to be very good at what he did.

Molly's Dad nodded. 'I might drop in on him over the weekend. See if I can help out with some of my contacts.'

'That would be good,' said Molly, not entirely sure what help her Dad would be, 'Joey would like that. You have to find Midnight for him.'

Molly's Dad smiled. 'I'll do what I can,' he said, opening the front door. 'Maria, we're home!' he called and

Molly's Mum appeared from the doorway joining the vets office to the house.

'I've just heard the news,' said Molly's Mum. 'Poor Joey,' she said, giving Molly a hug. 'I know how you must feel about this.'

Molly shrugged. 'Dad says he's going to help Sergeant Stopper find who did it and get Midnight back.'

Molly's Mum broke away from the hug. 'Can you do that?' she asked Molly's Dad.

Molly's Dad nodded. 'I said to Molly I'd see what I can do and I will, but after dinner. I've been cooking,' he said winking at Molly. 'Homemade steak pie and roasted vegetables.'

'I'd like it if you found Midnight more than eating dinner,' said Molly, untying her school tie and putting her jacket on one of the coat pegs by the front door. 'I'm going upstairs to get changed,' she said, before either of her parents could say anything.

When Molly came back downstairs, she wasn't the only person to have got changed. Her Mum was wearing her veterinary coat and was carrying a cup of tea from the kitchen into her office.

'Just a quick client to see,' said Molly's Mum. 'Help your Dad lay the table please.'

Molly stuck her head around the door. Her friend Ravi Sharma was sitting with his Mum. He was holding a small cardboard box with small circular holes cut at regular intervals at the top.

'Hello Dr Sharma,' said Molly's Mum. 'What can I do for Doris?'

Molly didn't wait to hear what was needed. She skipped into the kitchen, danced her way around her Dad collecting three plates, three sets of knives, forks and spoons. Molly took them into the dining room. She returned to collect three plates and ketchup. Then back again to bring in three glasses of water.

She arranged everything on the table exactly how her Mum usually arranged things on the table and lit the centrepiece candle just as they always did.

Molly's Dad brought the steak pie into the dining room. He came back a moment later with a ceramic dish filled with brightly coloured orange carrots, yellow sweetcorn, light green beans, dark green broccoli and clumps of white cauliflower. He set the dish down on one of the placemats and started serving generous portions of food onto the three plates.

Just as he finished, Molly's Mum returned. She looked a little sad and Molly gave her Mum a hug. She sat down and they started eating. Halfway through her first mouthful, Molly's Mum picked up her serviette and dabbed her eye.

What's wrong?' asked Molly.

'Doris,' said Molly's Mum. 'She was old, very old for a hamster and she's gone.'

Molly felt her own eyes prickle. 'Ravi's hamster is dead?' she whispered, knowing her Mum would have made certain of every possible treatment to keep the animal living longer but that sometimes it was kinder to choose the end. 'Poor Ravi,' she choked. 'First Joey's foal is stolen, now Ravi's hamster is dead.'

'She had a very happy life,' said Molly's Mum, 'you must remember that. I said exactly the same to Ravi. He was a very good owner. Very responsible. Always cleaned her cage when it needed doing and played with her every day. Apparently she used to spin in her wheel for hours while he was trying to sleep.'

Molly let out a small laugh. Ravi often looked tired. Perhaps that was why.

'I've given them the telephone number of a reputable hamster breeder. Ravi can contact them when and if the time is right for him to want to look after another one.'

'They only live for a few years,' said Molly's Dad. 'I had two when I was at school. It was always sad when they died but they were well looked after.'

Molly nodded. She knew all about the life cycle of animals, especially birds and small animals, from when she lived at her old home. Animals came into and out of her life frequently and she had learned to enjoy every moment with her friends.

Thinking of her friends reminded Molly of Bob. She was looking forward to chatting with him at bedtime. Hopefully he would have some news about Midnight.

When every plate was empty, Molly's Dad went into the kitchen. There was the sound of shuffling of tins and boxes in the cupboard, then he returned with a large three tier chocolate cake balanced on a plate in his hands.

'Surprise!' said Molly's Dad. 'As well as the homemade pie, I've made you both a cake!'

Molly squealed. 'Thank you! It's my favourite!'

Molly's Mum fetched a knife and cut the cake into neat slices. Chocolate oozed from the middle of the cake and Molly licked her lips. Soon half of the cake had been eaten and Molly was feeling rather full. It was getting late and she sensed her parents wanted some time together almost as much as she wanted to see Bob.

'Goodnight Molly,' said her parents and Molly said she'd see them in the morning.

Upstairs in her rooftop bedroom, Bob was already hopping from one leg to another on her windowsill.

'I thought you were never coming,' he grumbled. 'Huge servings of pie, chatter, chatter, chatter, then cake,' he said, looking at her reprovingly. 'Just because your Dad is home for a few days.'

Molly smiled and tipped out a handful of birdseed into Bob's saucer. 'My Dad is going to help find Midnight for Joey.'

Bob cocked his head, clearly considering this and weighing up in his mind whether that warranted eating chocolate cake or not.

'Very good Molly Manila,' said Bob. 'You may tell your Dad that Midnight was stolen by friends of Arabella Baxter to pay her debts and give her some money to move out of her family home. I can provide proof,' added Bob, seeing Molly give him a quizzical look.

'I'll need something more than telling my Dad a blue tit told me she did it,' said Molly, wishing it could be simple to share her knowledge. If her parents could talk to animals as well things would be so much easier.

'I'm not just "a blue tit" am I?' said Bob. If blue tits could look offended, Bob looked very offended and Molly sought to find the words to appease him.

'Of course you're not,' said Molly. 'But I need something to say so they know Arabella was behind this.'

Bob nodded his tiny head. 'I have just the thing,' he said, winking at Molly. 'Tomorrow morning, you must tell your Dad you heard Arabella talking about needing money and how much money horses are worth. You must convince your Dad to question Arabella and she will confess.'

Molly felt her mouth go dry. She had only just met Arabella. Joey's sister hadn't seemed to be one of the nicest of people, but could she really have done this?

'You can do this Molly Manila,' said Bob with great conviction. 'I believe in you,' he said, his mouth full of sunflower seeds.

'Thank you Bob,' said Molly, swapping her casual clothes for her pyjamas. She got into bed, words spinning around in her head, wondering exactly how to bring this up at breakfast tomorrow.

9

SOLVING PROBLEMS

Molly woke with sweat pouring down her face. She had been awake for much of the night worrying about Midnight and wondering how on earth she would talk to her Dad to help him ask the right questions of Arabella.

Molly put on her favourite jeans and a white blouse with a pattern of tiny red and blue flowers. She thought of what to say as she did up the buttons. She rehearsed the words inside her head and plodded slowly downstairs.

'Morning Molly,' said Molly's Mum as Molly arrived in the kitchen. 'Would you like a cup of tea? The kettle has just boiled.'

'Where's Dad?' asked Molly. 'He always makes the tea when he's home.'

'He's gone to see Sergeant Stopper,' said Molly's Mum. 'He couldn't sleep last night thinking about it.'

'Me neither,' muttered Molly, slightly annoyed all the words she'd thought of were now redundant. She would try and remember them for when he came home.

'I need you to get some things for me from the shops please,' said Molly's Mum. 'I've got some accounts to do this morning. I was going to do them next week but if your Dad is out this morning, you can run some errands, I can catch up on my paperwork and then we can spend the afternoon together.'

Molly nodded. She unclipped the shopping list from the magnet on the fridge door and scanned the items. She took the canvas bag and the money offered to her by her Mum.

'It's only a few things,' said Molly's Mum. 'You can buy yourself a magazine with the change if you like.'

'Please may I buy some birdseed instead?' asked Molly. 'I've been making friends with the birds in the garden and one of them comes onto my windowsill.'

'Of course,' said Molly's Mum. 'The change is all yours to spend on whatever you wish.'

Molly put on her shoes and coat and set off out of the house and down the road. She wondered if there would be time to see Casey and Jasmine. She knew their parents opened the fish and chip shop at the weekend and it was their busiest day.

Molly skipped down the street, the empty canvas shopping bag swinging wildly on her arm in time with her feet bouncing on the concrete pavement. She stopped outside Catch of the Day.

A sign on the door said "Closed until midday" so Molly peered through the window, hoping to see Jasmine or Casey in the kitchen behind the counter. They usually helped with cleaning and making sure any pre-ordered food was ready to be cooked.

Despite standing on her tiptoes and craning her neck, Molly couldn't see any movement or activity in the fish and chip shop at all.

Feeling a little disappointed, Molly walked the rest of the way to Mrs McGillam's village shop. She pushed open the door and a little bell chimed above her head.

Molly picked up a wire basket and checked the shopping list. She wandered around the shop picking up the items her Mum had requested. Molly added up the amounts as she put eggs, milk, bread, crisps, vegetables and biscuits into the basket. She stopped by the pet supplies and calculated that she could buy either a kilogram of peanuts or two kilograms of birdseed with the money left over from the family shopping.

Knowing how much Bob liked birdseed, she picked up the heavier bag and made her way over to where Mrs McGillam was waiting by the checkout till with her arms resting on the counter.

'That will be fifteen pounds exactly please,' said Mrs McGillam, holding out her hand for the money.

Molly smiled, she had added it up perfectly to the last penny, including Bob's birdseed. She checked her watch as she packed the groceries from the wire basket into her canvas bag. It was nearly midday and she wondered if Casey and Jasmine would be working yet.

'Thank you Molly,' said Mrs McGillam. 'It must be nice to have your Dad back.'

'Yes, Mrs McGillam,' said Molly. 'Oh,' she added, 'that's his car over by Catch of the Day. I'll go and meet him,' she said, slinging the canvas bag over her shoulder.

'Be careful of those eggs,' said Mrs McGillam, smiling as Molly turned on her heels and sped out of the shop.

Molly's Dad was in the car as Molly tapped on the window. He wound down the window and smiled at her.

'This was going to be a surprise,' said Molly's Dad. 'I was going to get us all fish and chips for lunch. I suppose now you're here you can come in and choose what you want.'

'Yes please,' said Molly. 'I also want to ask Casey and Jasmine something.'

Molly and her Dad went into Catch of the Day. Another small bell chimed as they opened the door and it chimed again as the door closed. Jasmine appeared from the kitchen wearing a green and yellow striped apron over dungarees and a purple tshirt.

'Hi Molly, hi Mr Manila,' said Jasmine, rubbing her hands on her apron. 'What can I get for you?'

'Two large cod and chips, one small cod and chips please,' said Molly's Dad. He looked at Molly and grinned. 'And two small sausages in batter, in a separate bag for the way home,' he added.

Molly beamed. 'You remembered!' she exclaimed, happy the tradition of something for the way home was being kept up.

'Coming right up,' said Jasmine. 'Twenty pounds please,' she added, shovelling freshly cooked chips into cardboard containers with a large handheld spade. Jasmine looked into one of the fryers underneath the glass counter. 'The fish will just be a couple of minutes.'

Molly sat on the waiting bench next to her Dad. Behind the counter she could see a digital clock with green numbers counting down and she guessed that's how long the fish would take.

'Did you check the fat containers?' asked Molly. 'Was that the cause of the problem? Mum hasn't had any sick cats or dogs for a few days.'

Jasmine nodded. 'I told my parents about it and they phoned the company who supplies the containers. It was really disgusting when they came to clean them, so bad they actually replaced all of the containers with brand new ones.'

'That's good news,' said Molly, making a mental note to tell Bob later. 'Hopefully no more animals will get sick.'

'That'll put your Mum out of business,' joked Molly's Dad. He took a twenty pound note out of his wallet as the numbers on the digital clock dropped to zero.

Jasmine placed the three pieces of cod into the cardboard boxes. She wrapped two small sausages in batter into two separate bags and handed everything to Molly.

'Thanks for calling in,' said Jasmine. 'See you at school on Monday.'

'Have you solved a problem Molly?' asked Molly's Dad.

Molly nodded. 'Cats and dogs were getting sick and it was because they were eating contaminated food out of the containers at the back of Catch of the Day.

'I've also solved a problem,' said Molly's Dad. 'I've found Midnight.'

'You found him!' exclaimed Molly. 'How? Where?'

'It turns out Lady Arabella and some of her friends took Midnight out into the field. She called it a dare, a prank, to take Joey's horse for a gallop around the field while Joey was asleep. However when they returned Midnight either she or one of her friends didn't bolt the stable door properly and Midnight let himself out. Apparently he tried to find Joey and get into the house, then wandered off down the driveway into another field.'

'Was he ok?' asked Molly. 'Did anything happen to him?'

'Midnight is fine,' said Molly's Dad. 'Joey is relieved and Lady Arabella has been spoken with. She won't be doing it again and her friends have been sent away.'

'What a horrible sister to have,' said Molly. 'No wonder Joey doesn't like her much.'

'Don't judge her too harshly,' said her Dad. 'You'll know what it's like to be eighteen soon enough. There's a rumour she's now dating a celebrity football player.'

'Well I hope I'm not like her,' said Molly, taking a bite of her sausage in batter.

Molly's Dad reversed the car into the space next to the front door, leaving the other spaces free for veterinary customers.

As soon as the engine stopped Molly jumped out and knocked on the door, impatient to get inside. Molly's Dad carried the canvas shopping bag, balanced the cardboard boxes of fish and chips in one hand and locked the car and tried to open the front door with his other hand.

As he was turning the key, the door opened with Molly's Mum pulling it as her Dad was pushing it. Everyone laughed and went inside.

Molly's Dad quickly put away the shopping and brought drinks out on to the patio where Molly and her Mum were laying out the boxes of fish and chips on the table in the garden.

'It's always nice to eat outside,' said Molly's Mum.

'Even better not to do any washing up,' said Molly's Dad.

Molly rolled her eyes. 'Where are we going this afternoon?' she asked, breaking up her parents romantic moment.

'We'll go out for a drive,' said Molly's Dad, 'find somewhere to stop, have a walk and enjoy some family time.'

Later in the evening, Molly fell asleep on the sofa while watching television with her parents. It had been an exhausting but fun afternoon with a short drive into the country, then hours walking through uneven fields filled with long grass, over wooden styles, crossing the river on narrow bridges, stopping in a pub for a drink, then repeating the walk, in reverse. All the fresh air had made Molly sleepy and coupled with a hot chocolate drink, she had rested her head on one of the lounge cushions and fallen fast asleep.

Molly woke up when her parents turned off the television. They had been watching a film sitting next to each other on the sofa on the other side of the room. Molly's Mum was resting her head against her Dad's shoulder and he was gently stroking her hair.

'I'm going to bed,' said Molly, stretching herself and standing up.

'Good night,' said her Mum and Dad in unison.

Molly gave them both a hug and went upstairs via the kitchen to collect the birdseed from Mrs McGillam's shop. As she hoped, Bob was perched on the windowsill. His head was tipped to one side as he looked expectantly up at her.

Molly took the two kilograms of birdseed out from behind her back. 'Surprise!' said Molly and she tipped two handfuls of seeds into Bob's saucer.

'Hello Molly Manila,' said Bob, his mouth full, dropping husks onto the windowsill. 'Midnight has been found,' he said, puffing his chest up with importance.

'I know,' said Molly, 'my Dad found him in one of the nearby fields. It sounds as though Lady Arabella and her friends didn't shut the stable door.'

'And the horse bolted,' finished Bob. 'I hope they gave her a strict telling off.'

'She won't be doing it again,' said Molly. 'Joey must be so happy.'

'He is,' said Bob. 'I saw him earlier. He took Midnight for a walk around the stables, tied him up outside while Joey mucked out his stall, got him fresh food and water, then spent nearly an hour brushing him and plaiting his tail.'

'Oh,' said Molly, feeling sorry she hadn't seen all of this. 'Joey is very good with horses. Also, I found out the problem with the fish and chip shop has been sorted out. No more cats and dogs will get sick from there.'

'I know,' said Bob, in the same tone of voice Molly had just used. 'I happened to be there when the company who supply the containers swapped them for new ones.'

'Oh,' said Molly. 'Well that's two problems sorted out,' she said, putting her hand over her mouth and yawning loudly. 'I wonder what tomorrow will bring.'

'Sunshine and showers,' said Bob, nodding his head knowledgably. 'Thank you for the seeds Molly Manila. Sleep well.'

10

ARCHIE IS NAUGHTY

Molly woke to the sound of Bob flapping around her face. She sneezed and held out her hand. Bob landed in her palm, a worried look on his face.

'What's the matter Bob?' asked Molly. 'Why are you here so early?'

'It is most certainly not early,' said Bob, 'and what's the matter is Archie. He has done something terribly naughty.'

Molly stifled a giggle. Archie the grumpy hedgehog, who she hadn't seen since her first day. The idea of him doing anything at all, let alone anything naughty wasn't something she had expected Bob to say.

'What has he done?' asked Molly, setting Bob down on her bedside chest of drawers.

'He's been very naughty,' said Bob, shaking his head, 'very, very naughty.'

'Yes, but what has he done?' asked Molly. 'If you don't tell me, I can't help.'

'It's too late to help,' said Bob. 'All too late.'

Molly pulled back her duvet and got out of bed. 'If you don't tell me what Archie has done and why it's too late to do anything then, well, I don't know Bob, I can't do anything,' she said, collecting her clothes and swapping her pyjamas for blue denim shorts and a pastel pink tshirt with a flamingo on the front.

'Archie has been bursting the tyres of all the bikes belonging to everyone in your class at school,' said Bob, puffing up his chest. 'Even yours.'

Molly put her hand over her mouth. 'Bursting all the tyres?' she exclaimed.

'Even your bike, not that I've seen you ride it yet,' said Bob. 'In fact, your tyres were the first he burst.'

'That's terrible,' said Molly. 'Why has he done that?'

'He said all the children are riding their bikes too fast,' said Bob. 'I tried to stop him, but he wasn't having any of it. He said he'd burst me next if I got in his way. It took him all night to do all the bikes in the village.'

'Oh Bob,' said Molly. 'I don't know if I can help with this.'

'Do what you always do Molly. I know you'll fix this. Perhaps go down and speak with Archie,' said Bob. 'He may listen to you.'

'What if he doesn't?' said Molly. 'How is anyone going to believe a hedgehog has done this? How am I supposed to explain why he has done this?'

'I know you will help Molly Manila,' said Bob winking at Molly.

'I'll do my best,' said Molly, her words falling in the empty room as Bob flew out of the open window.

After breakfast, Molly said she was going to play in the garden. This was fine with her parents as her Dad wanted to wash the car and her Mum wanted to write some letters. Molly slipped on her sandals and went out of the patio doors into the garden.

'Archie,' called Molly, 'Archimedes, are you there?' Still calling softly, Molly made her way to the overgrown path that ran down the side of the house. She knew hedgehogs usually liked to be tucked away out of sight. Archie was probably curled up in a ball. Molly bent down and gently sifted through the leaves.

After a few minutes shuffling slowly along the path, turning leaves over gently sifting them through her fingers she felt something firm and prickly. Delicately Molly pulled back the brambles and the top layer of leaves.

'Archie,' whispered Molly. 'Wake up, it's me, Molly. I need to talk to you.'

The prickly ball stayed firmly curled up. Archie was about twice the size of a tennis ball with thousands of needle sharp prickles protruding from everywhere. Molly gently rolled Archie over, looking for the tiny gap between his face and his feet.

'Archie,' she said again, her tone firmer as she grew impatient. 'Wake up. It's important.' She picked up a bramble and gently poked the prickles.

There was a low grumble and gradually the prickly ball got bigger and rounder, then thinner, then longer, until two little feet popped out of the front of the ball, followed by two more feet, a tummy and finally a pink nose with two beetle black eyes.

'What's important is sleep,' said Archie, looking extremely grumpy. 'I've been up all night. What do you want?'

'I want to know where you've been,' said Molly, putting her hands on her hips to show she meant business. 'I want to know if it's true that you have caused damage to my bike and my friends' bikes. I want…'

'I want. I want. I want,' grumbled Archie. 'I want some sleep. Go away,' he said starting to curl up again.

'Wait,' said Molly, desperately hoping Archie wouldn't refuse to speak with her. 'Please will you tell me if you burst the tyres on my bike?'

Archie looked directly at Molly and sniffed loudly. 'I am not talking to you or anyone else. I am going back to sleep. Please don't disturb me like that again.'

And with that, Archie scuffled the bundle of leaves into the air and curled himself up as they fell down like confetti around him.

No matter how many times Molly gently prodded him with the piece of bramble he didn't uncurl himself. In fact, he rolled deeper into the bushes out of Molly's reach.

'Well suit yourself,' said Molly. 'I'll find out myself,' and she stomped towards the garden shed where she knew her bike had been stored along with her helmet, lights and clip-on water bottle.

Molly swung the numbers around on the padlock to one, two, three, and unlocked the shed door. Inside was her shiny blue bike, but to her dismay, Molly could see that both tyres were completely flat. She spun the front tyre around and saw dozens of tiny puncture marks.

'Oh Archie,' said Molly as she checked the back tyre which had even more puncture holes. 'That's beyond repair,' said Molly, knowing even with bike glue and tape the rubber wheels would need replacing.

Feeling disappointed, Molly went back into the house. She met her Mum in the kitchen. Molly's Mum was busy sticking stamps on her letters. She looked up as Molly came in scuffing her feet on the floor.

'What's wrong?' asked Molly's Mum. 'Didn't you enjoy playing in the garden? You can invite some friends around this afternoon if you like.'

Molly sighed deeply. 'You won't believe me, but there's a hedgehog who's burst my bike tyres. They're both completely flat.'

Molly's Mum laughed, then stopped as she saw Molly was serious. 'A hedgehog you say?'

'Yes Mum, his name is Archimedes the Second but everyone calls him Archie,' said Molly.

'That's a very grand name for a hedgehog,' said Molly's Mum. 'How did he pop your tyres? With his spikes?' she laughed.

'That's right,' said Molly. 'But I know you don't believe me.'

'It is a little far fetched,' said Molly's Mum. 'But if your bike needs new tyres we can buy some. Have you tried repairing them?'

'There's no point,' Molly scowled. 'And it's not just my bike. Apparently, Archie has been all round the village bursting everyone's tyres.'

Molly's Mum chuckled. 'You have a vivid imagination.'

Molly shrugged. No-one ever believed her when she talked about her animal friends. Still, if Bob was right, she needed to help Archie, even if he didn't want her help.

'Hedgehogs,' grumbled Molly. She went up to her room to pack her schoolbag for Monday morning. She leaned out of the window, hoping to see Bob to tell him how Archie had been rude and ungrateful when she had tried to talk to him. But Bob didn't call round.

Instead, Molly had a visit from Joey and Lady Baxter. They stopped for a cup of tea and Lady Baxter could not thank Molly's Dad enough for finding Midnight and finding out Lady Arabella's involvement. They stayed for an hour, then Mr Tomkins returned in the silver Rolls Royce to collect them.

Molly walked slowly to school the following morning. She hadn't seen Bob and her Dad had left for another few weeks away shortly after having breakfast together.

Molly kicked at a stone on the pavement, then kicked it again, thinking of Jasmine who loved football, after a third kick the stone fell off the pavement and when Molly searched for it, the stone seemed to have fallen down a roadside drain and would never be seen again.

As Molly stepped back onto the kerb she felt a whooshing rush past her and Ravi and Robbie sailed past on their bikes.

'Hey!' shouted Molly as they whisked her homework papers out of her hands.

Robbie and Ravi just waved their hands over their shoulders and cycled on. Molly stopped to pick up her papers and carried on walking but also thinking that perhaps Archie had a point, the boys were riding a little bit too fast through the village.

Molly arrived at the school gates just as the bell rang for everyone to go inside. She hung up her jacket on her peg and Ravi came up to her.

'Sorry for knocking your papers,' said Ravi.

'You were going too fast,' said Molly, aware of how much she sounded like Archie. 'I thought everyone's tyres got burst.'

'They did,' said Ravi, looking serious. 'But Sargent Stopper fixed my bike and Robbie's bike yesterday. He had some spare tyres in his garage. There was no way they could be repaired.'

'My tyres got burst as well,' said Molly. 'I haven't even ridden my bike since I moved here.'

'That's not fair,' said Ravi. 'Maybe Robbie's Dad can fix your tyres for you.'

'Maybe,' said Molly. 'Does Sargent Stopper know who did it?'

Ravi burst into laughter. 'Robbie says his Dad said it was a hedgehog!'

'A hedgehog?' asked Molly.

'Seriously,' said Ravi. 'Ask him if you don't believe me,' and Ravi ran down the corridor and into the classroom.

Molly had to wait until break time to ask Robbie Stopper whether it was true.

At first Robbie didn't want to answer as he said it was his Dad's Police Business and Ravi shouldn't have told Molly clues about the case, but then he grinned and said he'd been allowed to watch the CCTV footage from outside Catch of the Day where Casey and Jasmine's bikes were chained to the front of the shop and in the middle of the night the camera picked up a hedgehog coming up to the bikes, shuffling around and then shuffling away.

'So it's not definite?' asked Molly. 'It might not have been a hedgehog.'

Robbie shook his head. 'It was definitely a hedgehog. After that, Dad watched the CCTV from other shops and the camera at the Post Office picked up a hedgehog coming out of one of the garden sheds where Luke McGillam keeps his bike.'

'Was it the same hedgehog? Maybe there was another one?' asked Molly, knowing in her heart that it was Archie and just Archie at work.

Robbie shrugged. 'What difference does it make? You can't prosecute a hedgehog. We'll just have to get our bikes fixed and hope it doesn't happen again.'

'I'll make sure it doesn't happen again,' Molly muttered under her breath. 'I'll chat to Archie when I get home and if he doesn't listen then I'll have to keep him awake until he does listen.'

The school day dragged slowly for Molly. She took notes in the History and Geography lessons, played Football in the Sports lesson and sang in tune in the Music lesson while her class learned new songs for the school pantomime for later in the year.

Molly's Mum was waiting at the school gates in her van. Molly's heart sank. She knew from experience it would be several hours before they would get home and it might be too dark to be allowed outside to search for a hedgehog.

'Where are we going?' asked Molly.

'We're going to Henley,' replied Molly's Mum. 'I've got a strange problem to help with. There's a cat that's got stuck in a catflap.'

11

FOOTBALL AT HENLEY

Molly giggled. 'Why have they called you?'

'It's not funny Molly,' said Molly's Mum. 'They've called me because I can help. It's also next to the football ground so I thought you might like to do a training session. Your friend Jasmine will be there and I've packed your sports kit in a bag in the back of the car.'

'Don't you want my help?' asked Molly.

'I'd rather you were busy with your friends. It might take a while to help free this cat and I thought you might enjoy playing football with Jasmine,' said Molly's Mum.

'Ok, said Molly. She reached for the sports bag and got out at the football stadium as her Mum parked the car.

'I'll just be over there,' said Molly's Mum, pointing to a red bricked terraced house with a blue front door in the middle of a row of red bricked houses. 'I'll come and find you in the stadium when I've finished.'

'Or when I'm finished,' muttered Molly, slinging the sports bag over her shoulder. 'See you soon Mum,' she said out loud, putting on a big smile, even though she wasn't looking forward to football training as much as she knew Jasmine would be.

Molly met Jasmine in the changing rooms. 'Hi Jasmine,' said Molly, unbuckling her school shoes and getting her sports kit out of her bag.

'Hi Molly!' said Jasmine, jumping up and giving Molly a hug. 'It's so cool you've come. They're doing try-outs tonight, talent spotting. You might get picked for the team!'

Jasmine's enthusiasm was infectious. Molly found herself smiling as she slipped on her shorts, tshirt, shinpads, long socks and trainers along with all the other girls in the changing rooms.

'Ready?' asked Jasmine, who had already started warming up by running on the spot.

'I'm ready,' laughed Molly and she skipped out of the changing rooms chatting away with Jasmine and the other girls.

After about half an hour of warming up and training drills, Molly noticed her Mum sitting in the stands. It looked as though she was holding a cat carrying basket and Molly wondered whether it was the cat that had got stuck and whether the cat would be coming home with them.

Another half an hour later and Molly was dripping with sweat. She had run the length of the pitch more times than she could count. She had passed balls, kicked long distance balls, practiced penalties and even had a go in goal as the goalkeeper.

Jasmine Cooper had been much better than Molly but she had actually really enjoyed herself. Molly and Jasmine stopped to see Molly's Mum at the end of the session.

'Hello Mrs Manila,' said Jasmine. 'Molly was amazing tonight!'

'I was watching,' said Molly's Mum. 'I hope you enjoyed it Molly. You can come next week if you like.'

Molly's eyes lit up. 'Yes please,' she said.

'I've also been given something very exciting,' said Molly's Mum, reaching into her coat pocket. 'The owner of the cat has given me a dozen tickets to watch Henley City play next weekend. I wondered if you'd like to get some friends together and go to the match.'

'Wow,' said Molly, looking at the large cat basket and wondering what type of cat was inside and why the owner had not only given away their cat but also several hundreds of pounds worth of football tickets.

'Thank you Mrs Manila,' said Jasmine. 'I'll ask my parents if Casey and I can go.'

'You're welcome,' Molly's Mum smiled, 'I'm sure you'll have a lovely time.'

Molly and Jasmine got changed at lightning speed. Mrs Cooper was waiting in the car park as Jasmine, Molly and her Mum left the stadium. Jasmine held up the tickets and showed her Mum.

Mrs Cooper laughed and nodded. 'Of course you can go. We'll be there anyway to provide takeaway fish and chips so it won't be a problem.'

'What's wrong with the cat?' asked Molly as they turned out of the football stadium car park. 'How come you're looking after it?'

'The owner is going on holiday for a week. They want me to put the cat on a diet,' explained Molly's Mum.

At the word "diet" the basket rocked backwards and forwards. Even though the basket was in the back of the car, Molly heard a distinct grumbling from the cat muttering and mumbling about how much it liked fresh fish and food was the only thing it looked forward to in the day.

'The cat is probably bored,' said Molly. 'Is it kept inside all day?'

'Only since he grew too big for the catflap,' said Molly's Mum. 'They don't want a bigger hole in the door, so the cat needs to be smaller. Looking at the size of him, I think he's probably eaten everything inside the house. Staying with us for a few days will help get him back in shape.'

Molly nodded. 'What's his name?' she asked.

'Henley,' said Molly's Mum. 'I think he must be named after the football club.'

A few days later Henley was certainly slimmer. He spent most of his time in the kitchen looking hopefully at anyone who came into the room in case they dropped titbits or crumbs. But Molly knew better than to feed him and she resisted Henley's purring and weaving around her ankles.

Molly also learned very quickly to keep her bedroom door shut. After a heated conversation with an outraged Bob who had come to check for his evening meal and nearly been attacked, Molly knew she could take no chances with her animal friends trying to eat each other.

So Henley was allowed in the kitchen, the lounge and the first floor bedrooms but not into Molly's attic room.

'I'm sorry Henley,' said Molly as she shuffled the cat away from her bedroom door. 'I'll see you in the morning,' she promised and clicked the door shut.

Henley had only scratched her door on his first night. Then Molly learned he had taken it upon himself to sleep at the foot of her Mum's bed. Probably hoping her Mum would feed him in her sleep, Molly thought to herself.

Molly scooped some birdseed into Bob's saucer and waited for him to perch himself on her windowsill. She didn't have to wait long as with the fluttering of wings Bob landed neatly by the saucer and pecked at the seed.

'Thank you Molly Manila,' said Bob, his mouth full and dropping the husks as he spoke. 'How long is that cat staying?' he grumbled.

'Two more days,' said Molly smiling at Bob. 'He's a nice cat really.'

Bob shook his head. 'If you're a bird then there's no such thing as a nice cat,' he said matter of factly. 'Everyone knows that.'

'I disagree,' said Molly, topping up the saucer with seed. The packet was nearly empty and she made a mental note to buy some more at the weekend when her Mum asked her to get the food shopping.

'I suppose he's staying until that football match,' said Bob. 'Funny game just kicking a ball around.'

'It's good fun,' said Molly. 'Jasmine's really good at it.'

Bob lifted one of his toes and flicked one of the husks. It sailed into the air and landed at Molly's feet.

'I suppose there's some fun to be had if you play,' said Bob, flicking another husk into the air.

'Hey!' laughed Molly. 'I'll have to pick these up you know.'

Bob nodded. 'Sorry Molly Manila,' he said, kicking one last husk into the air and nudging it with his head. 'I might take up playing football one day.'

Molly laughed again. 'I don't think birds can play football.'

Bob shrugged. 'I only said I might,' he said, looking a little offended. 'Anyway, have you been listening to the news?'

Molly shook her head. 'What news?'

'A famous footballer is going to be at the match. One of Lady Arabella Baxter's friends,' said Bob nodding enthusiastically. 'He is well known for his donations to animal welfare charities.'

'How do you know all this?' laughed Molly. 'More importantly, why are you telling me?'

'For your Mum,' said Bob. 'When you are at the football game you need to tell him your Mum is a vet and that she has a new animal sanctuary project coming up. He will give you something valuable in return. You must also be careful when tying your shoelaces.'

'My shoelaces?' asked Molly. 'What have you done to my shoelaces?'

'Wait and see Molly Manila,' said Bob. 'You will find out everything at the football match. Please make sure that cat does not come back. I have a family in the garden and we do not like cats nearby.'

Molly nodded. 'I thought you might have a family.'

Bob puffed up his chest. 'I have a very big family. Soon it will be even bigger.'

'I'd like to meet them one day,' said Molly. 'When they can fly. I will get another saucer and have all the birdseed they can eat.'

'Thank you Molly, that is very kind,' said Bob, hopping from one foot to the other. 'As their Dad, I will teach them how to take food from you and also how to find food in the garden as well.'

'I would like that very much,' said Molly.

'All in good time,' said Bob, 'and if it doesn't happen, then you will know that it was for a good reason. Sometimes it is time to move on.'

Molly nodded, her eyes closing. 'All for a good reason,' she murmured as she drifted off to sleep.

12

TIME TO MOVE ON

Molly woke early in the morning. Thoughts of the football match were buzzing in her head. Who would the celebrity be and how could she meet him to tell him all about her Mum and the vet services she provided?

She dressed in her Henley City football top and matching shorts, pulled up her socks and slipped on her trainers. Both her parents were waiting for her downstairs.

Molly talked nineteen to the dozen about the game and the players she was looking forward to meeting.

'Did you know Oz Bridges is going to be there?' asked Molly's Mum. 'He's been in the news recently.'

'Is he famous?' asked Molly.

'Very famous,' laughed Molly's Mum. 'He does a lot of work looking after sick and injured animals.'

'Do you think he could help you at the vets?' asked Molly.

Molly's Mum nodded. 'It would be lovely to have his support and maybe he would like to be involved in something I'm hoping to create alongside the vets.'

'Like what? asked Molly. 'Will you set up a new animal sanctuary?'

Molly's Mum laughed. 'How did you know about that? I haven't even told your Dad yet!'

Molly grinned. 'I heard about it from a little bird.'

Molly's Dad laughed. 'Was it from that blue tit that eats the sunflower seeds from your bedroom windowsill?'

Molly nodded, even though she knew neither of her parents would believe her.

'What time can we go?' asked Molly. She felt anxious to make sure they arrived in time to meet Oz Bridges so she could ask him about Bob's plan for her to chat with him about the animal sanctuary. 'Jasmine and Casey should be here soon.'

No sooner had she said the words, the doorbell rang and Molly leapt out of her seat.

'Jasmine! Casey!' she yelled as her friends burst through the door. 'Mum! They're here!'

With a hustle and bustle Molly, her Mum, Jasmine and Casey and all their bags for the day were loaded into Molly's Mum's car and they set off.

The journey was easy and they arrived in the car park in plenty of time. Molly's Mum handed some coins to the lady in a yellow jacket collecting money for charity at the entrance and handed over their tickets.

'You've got the best seats at the game,' said the lady in the yellow jacket.

Molly grinned as she heard the lady say exactly the same thing to the family behind them. She scurried up the steps to find their row of seats and flung herself into the aisle seat so she could leap up when the players came out of the tunnel.

As the stadium filled the noise grew louder and louder. Team chants broke out and Molly joined in shouting "Henley! Henley! Henley!" at the top of her voice. She felt a sharp nudge in her ribs. Jasmine had poked her hard.

'Look!' hissed Jasmine. 'It's Dean, Kipper, Marco, Favin and Oz coming out onto the pitch.'

Molly looked as the players walked out onto the grass and took up their positions. She could see a man with "Bridges" on his back take up the position in the goal furthest away from their seats.

'That's him,' Molly whispered.

'That's who?' asked Jasmine.

'Oz,' replied Molly. 'I have to speak with him after the game.'

Jasmine laughed. 'You've got no chance! The players go into the clubhouse at the end and no one gets to go in there unless you're a VIP.'

'A what?' asked Molly.

'A Very Important Person, a celebrity or something,' said Jasmine sadly. 'You need to be famous to go in there on a match day.'

Molly nodded, her brain whirring thinking of elaborate plans to break into the clubhouse and demand to speak with the goalkeeper. A loud whistle broke her thoughts.

Jasmine leapt up in her seat as the ball was kicked long and hard towards the Henley goal. Moments later she sank back into the plastic chair as the ball was caught and thrown back to a Henley defender and passed back up the pitch.

Molly found herself swept up in the game, cheering for Henley and keeping a close eye on the ball trying to second guess which player would receive it, almost like a game of chess trying to outwit the opponents several moves ahead.

The half time whistle blew and Mr Wicket from school jogged out onto the pitch. Molly hadn't seen him on the benches below their seats. He had a megaphone and before

Molly realised she was being hoisted out of her seat by an excited Jasmine.

'Come on!' shrieked Jasmine. 'We get to play a quick game at half time!'

Molly scrambled down the steps as fast as her feet would carry her. Ravi, Robbie and Abigale were already beside the team benches getting autographs. A red bib was flung over Molly's head and she was ushered onto the pitch.

'Get ready,' said Mr Wicket and he threw a football at Casey's feet. 'You've got five minutes to score as many goals as you can.'

'No way!' shouted Casey. 'Look who's in goal!'

'Oz Bridges,' said Molly suddenly remembering Bob's instructions. 'How am I supposed to say anything?' she wondered.

Jasmine grabbed Molly's elbow. 'Come on!'

Molly jogged up the pitch barely hearing the crowd cheering as Robbie took the first kick from the penalty spot. The ball sailed over the top of the goal. Oz Bridges went up to Robbie and gave him a high five.

Casey was next. He took a long run up and kicked the ball as hard as he could. There was a loud clang as the ball ricocheted off the post.

'Good try,' said Oz Bridges, coming out of the goal to give Casey a high five.

Jasmine looked nervous as she approached the goal at a jog, taking her time and giving the ball a perfectly timed kick. There was another clang as the ball hit the same post and bounced away into the crowd. She high fived Oz Bridges and walked back to the halfway line.

'Aim a bit lower,' Jasmine said to Molly. 'There's a gap under where Robbie missed.'

Molly nodded and took the ball in both hands. She laid it on the penalty spot and started her run up. As she approached, her right shoe felt loose, she looked down and the shoelace had come undone. The crowd cheered and Molly saw her Mum standing up to watch. There was no time to stop. She ran towards the ball and swung her right foot back

Suddenly the ground and the sky switched places and Molly felt herself flying through the air in a somersault. She landed on her back and gasped as the wind was knocked out of her. There was an even louder gasp from the crowd, a murmur of laughter and then a deathly silence.

Four medics streamed onto the pitch, one stopping at Molly and the others running towards the goal.

'I'm ok,' said Molly as a woman in a yellow jacket helped her to her feet. 'I slipped. Honestly, I'm ok.'

Molly brushed herself down and walked with the lady across the pitch to a volley of applause from the crowd. She found herself walking lopsidedly and looked down. Her right shoe was missing.

'Where's my shoe?' Molly asked the lady in the yellow jacket. 'I had it on just now but the lace was undone.'

'It flew off your foot as you kicked the ball,' said the lady in the yellow jacket. 'It hit Oz Bridges in the face. It looks like he's ok though,' she added as Molly gasped.

'Oh no,' said Molly. 'I'm so sorry. Will he be ok?'

The lady in the yellow jacket nodded. 'I'm sure he'll be fine. You can ask him yourself at the end of the match. Yours was the only penalty that went in, so you've won the prize to meet the players.'

'Meet the players?' Molly choked on the words, her mind a whirl of embarrassment and excitement at the opportunity to ask about the animal sanctuary.

'You'll get to meet all the players, have a drink with them, a soft drink mind, and get any autographs you want,' said the lady in the yellow jacket. 'If you're sure you're ok, go back to your seat, enjoy the second half and we'll find you at the end of the game.'

Molly tried to ignore all the people looking at her. She watched as Abigale took her penalty. Oz Bridges had a bandage on his cheek. The ball went wide and Molly clapped as Abigale shrugged and came to join Molly, Casey and Jasmine in their seats.

'I can't go and meet him afterwards,' Molly whispered to Jasmine. 'I'm so embarrassed.'

Jasmine grinned. 'It's ok, we can all go. Mr Wicket has arranged for everyone who took penalties to go into the clubhouse, so you won't be on your own.'

Molly breathed a huge sigh of relief. 'That's ok then,' she said and slumped back into her seat.

Two goals were scored and the Henley City stand erupted in an enormous cheer as the final whistle blew. The winning result would mean they qualified to play in the higher division next season. Molly cheered and clapped until her throat was dry and her hands were sore.

As the crowd cleared the lady in the yellow jacket came to find them.

'Come and meet the players,' the lady in the yellow jacket said with a smile, 'they're looking forward to meeting you,' she added, handing Molly her missing shoe.

'Especially Molly!' laughed Jasmine. 'I bet that's never happened before!'

The lady in the yellow jacket laughed. 'Not that I can remember!' She guided the party of children and Molly's Mum into the foyer of the clubhouse.

Molly stared at the large portraits on the walls, felt her feet sink into the thick carpet and followed Jasmine and

Casey into a room with "Players Only" written on a plaque on the door.

Oz Bridges was sitting on a wooden bar stool, one hand clasped around his drink and the other hand entwined with a woman's hand. As Molly approached him, she realised it was Lady Arabella's hand and she was sitting next to Oz Bridges with Joey on her other side.

'Hi Joey,' said Molly, her nerves fading as Joey flashed her a grin.

'I saw your penalty,' said Joey. 'We were up in the sponsor's box. It was going in even if your shoe hadn't come off and hit Oz.'

Hearing his name, Oz Bridges turned around. Molly felt her knees wobble.

'I'm so sorry,' Molly stuttered. 'It was an accident.'

Oz threw back his head and laughed, his infectious chuckle louder than the music playing and his teammates turned to look. Some of them came over and Molly blushed.

'I should have checked my laces,' said Molly.

'It was a great goal, wasn't it Oz?' said Joey.

'Absolutely,' Oz agreed. 'If you don't get signed for Henley City, come and join our club when you're older.'

'Please may I get your autograph?' asked Jasmine.

'Me too,' said Casey.

'And me,' added Abigale.

'Sure,' said Oz, reaching into his pocket for a pen.

Jasmine produced a sports magazine and turned to a full page picture of Oz and his team. A squiggle later and she was beaming.

'I'll get you all some tickets for our next game,' said Oz.

'Thank you!' said Jasmine.

'Thank you!' said Casey, Robbie and Ravi.

Lady Arabella nudged Joey and Joey winked at Molly.

'Let's go and get some drinks,' said Joey. He stepped down from his bar stool and linked arms with Jasmine and Casey leading them away from the players. Robbie, Ravi and Abigale followed, leaving Molly a couple of paces behind them. Lady Arabella gave Molly a frosty stare.

'I just have a quick question,' said Molly. 'Then you can be alone again.'

Oz Bridges grinned at Molly. 'What is it?' he asked.

Molly took a deep breath and poured out how her Mum was the village vet, all about the animals she helped and her Mum's plan to set up the animal sanctuary to give treatment and a home to sick and injured creatures.

Before she had finished speaking Oz was nodding. Lady Arabella was nodding and so were several of Oz's team. Oz waved at Molly's Mum and beckoned her over.

Molly took a couple of steps backwards and left her Mum to chat with the football stars. She stayed with her friends drinking lemonade and eating chips from a large basket brought to them by the man behind the bar.

Molly kept glancing across and each time she was pleased to see that Oz, Lady Arabella and her Mum were deep in conversation.

Eventually Molly's Mum stood up, shook hands with Oz and Lady Arabella. She came over to Molly's table of friends with a big smile.

'Thank you Molly,' said Molly's Mum. 'I'm so glad you didn't tie your shoelace properly!'

It was late when they returned home. Molly was over the moon that she'd had the chance to meet Oz Bridges. He was the nicest person she'd ever met.

Oz was going to help many sick and injured animals and both Molly and her Mum were sure he would convince Lady Arabella to help him.

With celebrity support, the animal sanctuary at Stags Farm would provide shelter and treatment for any creature great or small that needed help. Molly's Mum would run the centre and Molly would help after school and at weekends.

A black van was parked outside Molly's house and all the lights were turned on inside the house. Molly felt scared. Her Mum squeezed Molly's hand.

'I thought this might happen,' said Molly's Mum.

'What's going on?' whispered Molly. 'Is everything ok?'

Molly's Dad met them at the front door. He was dressed in a suit and took both Molly and her Mum by the hand.

'I've got something to tell you both,' said Molly's Dad. 'I hope it will be ok.'

'What is it?' asked Molly. 'What's happened?'

Molly's Dad smiled. 'It's nothing to worry about. I've got a new boss,' said Molly's Dad. 'He's moving my team.'

'But why can't we stay here?' asked Molly, clutching at his arm, begging him to change his mind.

'You didn't want to come,' reminded Molly's Mum. 'You wanted to stay at our old home, but you found new friends and made a fresh start. You can do it again.'

'I don't want to,' wept Molly. 'All my friends are here.'

Her Dad looked sadly at Molly. 'I know it's hard.'

'You don't have to make new friends,' said Molly. 'Everyone you know is going with you.'

'I have to make new friends,' said Molly's Mum. 'It's not easy for me either.'

Molly nodded. 'I knew we were going to have to go at some point. Bob told me,' Molly added under her breath and because Bob had told her first, she knew it was true.

A few days later the removal vans arrived. Molly watched as the boxes were loaded carefully one by one into the back of two large grey removal vans. She sat in the back garden looking at the flowerpot where she had planted the acorn on the day they had arrived in Greentrees.

The acorn had grown into a small tree that had outgrown its pot. The roots were spilling out of the sides and Molly felt the same. She had outgrown her home in Greentrees. Molly had arrived with a purpose to help the animals in the village and she had achieved that goal.

The animal sanctuary at Stags Farm would be built next year. Lady Arabella and Oz Bridges would run it and they'd promised Molly could visit whenever she wanted.

All of her goodbyes had been said.

Everyone had cried a few tears, but there had been smiles and laughter as Molly recounted all the problems she had helped to solve.

As her parents got into the car, Molly looked out of the window. She could see her old bedroom window that looked out over the driveway. She smiled as she saw Bob with a female blue tit and five small blue tits. He had his family and she had hers.

'I will come back,' said Molly, her eyes watering for the hundredth time. 'I promise I'll come back soon.'

The End.

Find your next reading adventures at

www.mollymanila.com

www.sammyrambles.com

www.bumperandfriends.com

Printed in Great Britain
by Amazon

79136486R00092